CHRISTMAS CROCHET
FOR HEARTH, HOME & TREE

Christmas Crochet

for HEARTH, HOME & TREE

Stockings, Ornaments, Garlands and More

EDIE ECKMAN

Storey Publishing

The mission of Storey Publishing is to serve our customers by
publishing practical information that encourages
personal independence in harmony with the environment.

Edited by Gwen Steege and Karen Manthey
Art direction and book design by Jessica Armstrong
Text production by Liseann Karandisecky
Indexed by Eileen Clawson

Cover and interior photography by © Alexandra Grablewski, except
    pages 5, 45–48, 88–92, 138, 146, and 158–165 by Mars Vilaubi
Illustrations by Katrina Loving
Pattern charts by Karen Manthey

Storey Publishing
210 MASS MoCA Way
North Adams, MA 01247
www.storey.com

Printed in the United States by Versa Press
10   9   8   7   6   5   4   3   2   1

Library of Congress Cataloging-in-Publication Data

Eckman, Edie.
  Christmas crochet for hearth, home & tree / by Edie Eckman.
    pages cm
  Includes index.
  ISBN 978-1-61212-329-5 (pbk. : alk. paper)
  ISBN 978-1-61212-330-1 (ebook) 1. Crocheting. 2. Christmas stockings.
    3. Christmas tree ornaments. I. Title.
TT820.E348 2014
746.43'4—dc23
                                                2014020889

For Crocheters

who celebrate the holiday season
in whatever form it takes.

Contents

Welcoming the Holidays

WHETHER YOU CELEBRATE CHRISTMAS for religious or secular reasons, chances are it's your favorite holiday. It's so easy to get into the spirit of the season when you see the lights and decorations that spring up in stores and on the streets, sometimes as early as October.

What could be better than combining a favorite holiday with a favorite pastime? The eighteen projects in *Christmas Crochet* include plenty of the primo Christmas project — stockings — as well as tree and home decorations. Most of the projects use relatively small amounts of yarn, and many are perfect for using up odd balls from your existing yarn stash.

Some guest designers have joined me to offer their take on Christmas décor. Kristin Omdahl's angelic ornaments, Andee Graves's adorable birds, Barbara Kreuter's bows and freeform(ish) stocking, and Carol Ventura's unique personalized tapestry crochet stocking round out a collection that has something for everyone. Their projects are credited with their names; all other designs are my own.

We offer a range of crochet techniques, from the most basic double-crochet circles to novel stitch patterning, tapestry crochet, and Tunisian techniques. Newer crocheters will delight in whipping up the easy Felted Ornaments (page 84), while more advanced crocheters will enjoy exploring new techniques with the Candy Cane Stocking (page 70). Different yarn weights are also represented, from crochet thread through worsted-weight yarn.

Patterns best suited for less-confident crocheters are marked as "easy"; crocheters of all skill levels can identify any beyond-the-basics techniques used by scanning the Pattern Essentials section at the beginning of each pattern. If you see a skill you don't know yet, don't panic. We've written the pattern as clearly as possible to walk you through each step of the way. Don't shy away from adventure; try something new!

So whether it's July and you are looking for warm-weather projects, or it's late November and you need to crochet some quick gifts, you'll find projects here to delight and inspire.

IMAGINE COLOR. While Christmas red and green are always safe colors, don't hesitate to choose modern brights or neutrals for an updated look. In most projects you aren't committing to a lot of stitching. Use your imagination to see the projects in your favorite colorway, to fit right at home with you!

USE YOUR STASH. The yarns specified are classic and easily found in your local yarn shop. If you have yarn in your stash that you'd prefer to substitute, we've made that easy to do. Refer to the yarn weight classification in each project, and to the chart on page 179 of the appendix to help you choose wisely.

GET EXACT GAUGE . . . OR NOT. In many projects, gauge is not critical. However, it is a good starting point for determining the finished size of the piece, the amount of yarn needed, and the drape of the fabric you are creating. If you don't care about the finished size, and you have plenty of yarn and are getting a crocheted fabric that is neither too loose nor too stiff, don't worry about matching the gauge of the pattern.

CROCHET TO A SYMBOL CHART. Many crocheters prefer to work from a symbol chart, so when possible we've included those in addition to the text instructions. You'll find a key to the symbols, as well as a list of abbreviations and glossary, in the appendix.

FOR YOU "LEFTIES." Instructions are written for right-handed cro-cheters [with instructions for left-handed crocheters in brackets]. Left-handers may follow the same stitch diagrams, reading in the direction of the stitching.

For the
Hearth

Mix-and-Match Stockings

ONE PATTERN + FOUR COLORS = MAKE IT YOUR OWN. From color combinations to embellishments, this stocking pattern is an empty palette for creating your own style. The stitch pattern is easy enough to memorize and creates its own rhythm. It's fun to use the mix-and-match concept to see how many different color combos/patterns can be generated from so little yarn. Four balls of yarn made three complete stockings, with yarn left over.

FINISHED MEASUREMENTS

▶ 13"/33 cm in circumference, 19"/48.5 cm long

YARN

▶ Brown Sheep Nature Spun (4), 100% wool, 245 yds/224 m, 3.5 oz/100 g, 1 skein each Colors 109 Spring Green (A), N78 Turquoise Wonder (B), N85 Peruvian Pink (C), and 740 Snow (D)

CROCHET HOOK

▶ US H/8 (5 mm) *or size needed to obtain correct gauge*

GAUGE

▶ 14½ sts and 10 rnds = 4"/10 cm in stitch pattern

OTHER SUPPLIES

▶ Yarn needle

OPPOSITE PAGE, FROM LEFT TO RIGHT: Stocking #1, Stocking #3, Stocking #2.

PATTERN ESSENTIALS

sc2tog (single crochet 2 stitches together)
(Insert hook into next st and pull up a loop) two times,
yarnover and pull through all 3 loops on hook.

sc3tog (single crochet 3 stitches together)
(Insert hook into next st and pull up a loop) three times,
yarnover and pull through all 4 loops on hook.

sc-dec (single crochet decrease)
Into the 2 stitches indicated, insert hook from front to back through
first stitch and from back to front through 2nd stitch, yarnover
and pull up a loop, yarnover and pull through both loops.

standing sc (standing single crochet)
Beginning with slip knot on hook, insert hook into stitch indicated,
yarnover, pull up a loop, yarnover and pull through both loops on hook.

working into back bump of chain
With the wrong side of the chain facing, insert hook into the bumps on
the back of the chain. (The right side of the chain is a series of Vs.)

• PROJECT NOTES •

▶ All the stockings are worked using the
same basic pattern, with variations for
color and cuff choices (see page 18 for
variations).

▶ Stocking is worked in the round from the
top down, with an opening made for the
heel. The heel is worked after the foot and
toe are complete.

▶ Change to new color on the last slip stitch
of the previous round as directed.

STITCH PATTERN

RNDS 1, 3, AND 5: Ch 1, sc in each st around, join with slip st to first sc.

RNDS 2 AND 4: Ch 3 (counts as dc), dc in each st around, join with slip st to top of ch-3.

Rep Rnds 1–5 for stitch pattern.

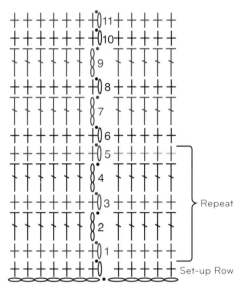

CUFF AND LEG

Basic Stocking

CUFF AND LEG

▸ With cuff color, ch 46, join with slip st to form a ring, being careful not to twist chain.

SETUP RND: Ch 1, sc in each ch around, join with slip st to first sc. (46 sc)

▸ Beginning with Rnd 1 of Stitch Pattern, work 5 repeats (25 rounds), changing colors as directed (see Color & Cuff Variations on page 18), until piece measures approx. 10"/25 cm from beginning, ending with Rnd 5 of stitch pattern. Fasten off.

DIVIDE FOR HEEL: With heel color, place a slip knot on hook, leaving a 6"/15 cm tail, skip 35 sc, slip st in back loop of next sc, ch 23, skip 23 sc, slip st in back loop of next sc. Fasten off, leaving a 6"/15 cm tail.

FOOT

▸ With heel color, working into back bump of chain, standing sc in 11th ch, sc in remaining 12 chs, sc in next st (same st as slip st), sc in next 22 dc, sc in each remaining ch, join with slip st to first sc. (46 sc)

▸ Continuing in established stitch and color pattern, work three pattern repeats as established; foot measures approximately 6"/15 cm from chain. Fasten off, leaving a 6"/15 cm tail.

TOE

RND 1: With toe color, ch 1, sc in each sc around, join with slip st to first sc. (46 sc)

RND 2: Ch 1, sc in next 2 sc, *sc-dec, sc in next 2 sc; rep from * around, join with slip st in first sc. (35 sc)

RNDS 3, 5, AND 7: Ch 1, sc in each st around, join with slip st to first sc.

RND 4: Ch 1, *sc-dec, sc in next 3 sc; rep from * around, join with slip st to first sc. (28 sc)

RND 6: Ch 1, *sc in next 2 sc, sc-dec; rep from * around, join with slip st to first sc. (21 sc)

RND 8: Ch 1, *sc-dec, sc in next sc; rep from * around, join with slip st to first sc. (14 sc)

RND 9: Ch 1, (sc2tog) around, join with slip st to first sc. (7 sc)

▸ Fasten off, leaving a 6"/15 cm tail. Thread yarn tail through remaining sts and pull tight to close hole.

HEEL

RND 1: With heel color and right side facing, standing sc in first st of round (back heel), sc in next 9 sc, sc3tog in next 2 sts and next ch, sc in next 20 ch, sc3tog in next ch and next 2 sc, sc in next 10 sc, join with slip st to first sc. (42 sc)

RND 2: Ch 1, sc in next 9 sc, sc3tog, sc in next 18 sc, sc3tog, sc in next 9 sc, join with slip st to first sc. (38 sc)

RND 3: Ch 1, sc in next 8 sc, sc3tog, sc in next 16 sc, sc3tog, sc in next 8 sc, join with slip st to first sc. (34 sc)

RND 4: Ch 1, sc in next 7 sc, sc3tog, sc in next 14 sc, sc3tog, sc in next 7 sc, join with slip st to first sc. (30 sc)

RND 5: Ch 1, sc in next 6 sc, sc3tog, sc in next 12 sc, sc3tog, sc in next 6 sc, join with slip st to first sc. (26 sc)

RND 6: Ch 1, sc in next 5 sc, sc3tog, sc in next 10 sc, sc3tog, sc in next 5 sc, join with slip st to first sc. (22 sc)

RND 7: Ch 1, sc in next 4 sc, sc3tog, sc in next 8 sc, sc3tog, sc in next 4 sc, join with slip st to first sc. (18 sc)

RND 8: Ch 1, sc in next 3 sc, sc3tog, sc in next 6 sc, sc3tog, sc in next 3 sc, join with slip st to first sc. (14 sc)

RND 9: Ch 1, *sc2tog, rep from * around. (7 sc)

▸ Fasten off, leaving an 8"/20.5 cm tail. Thread tail through outside loop of remaining 7 scs. Pull tail to inside and draw tight to close the hole.

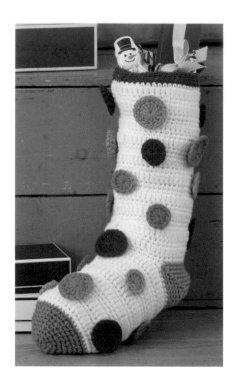

EDGING

RND 1: With edging color and RS facing, standing sc in first foundation chain at center back leg, sc in each foundation ch around, join with slip st to first sc. (46 sc)

RND 2: Ch 8 or desired length for hanging loop, sc in each sc around, join with slip st to first sc.

▸ Fasten off.

FINISHING

▸ Use yarn tails at heel corners to close any existing gaps. Weave in all ends.

Color & Cuff Variations

STOCKING #1

▸ First cuff color and set-up rnd, heel color, toe color: C

▸ Stripe Pattern: All sc rnds in B, all dc rnds in A

▸ Edging color: C

STOCKING #2

▸ First cuff color and set-up rnd: B

▸ Stripe Pattern: *C C D C C B B D B B; rep from * throughout.

▸ Heel, toe, and edging color: A

STOCKING #3

- ▸ First cuff color, set-up rnd, and edging color: C

- ▸ Heel color: A

- ▸ Toe color: B

- ▸ Remainder of stocking: D

- ▸ Circles: A, B, and C

LARGE CIRCLE

- ▸ Make 3 in A, 3 in B, 6 in C.

- ▸ Leave a 6"/15 cm tail for sewing, begin with sliding loop.

RND 1: Ch 3 (counts as dc), 11 dc in ring, join with slip st to top of ch-3. (12 dc)

RND 2: Ch 1, *sc in next sc, 2 sc in next sc; rep from * around, join with slip st to first sc. (18 sc)

- ▸ Fasten off, leaving a 6"/15 cm tail for sewing.

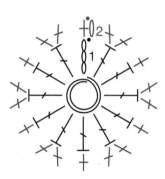

LARGE CIRCLE

SMALL CIRCLE

- ▸ Make 6 in A, 6 in B, 3 in C

- ▸ Work as for Large Circle through Rnd 1. Fasten off.

SMALL CIRCLE

FINISHING

- ▸ Arrange circles in a pleasing pattern on main portion of stocking leg and foot.

- ▸ Sew center of circles to stocking using yarn tails. If desired, sew outer edges of circles to stocking. Weave in ends.

Colorful Stripes Stocking

THE BRIGHT COLORS IN THIS STRIPED STOCKING are reminiscent of old-fashioned ribbon candy. Single crochet stitches worked in the back loops throughout create a unique pattern and texture. This stocking offers the perfect opportunity to use up odd balls of yarn and practice your stripe-making at the same time.

FINISHED MEASUREMENTS

▸ 12½"/32 cm in circumference, 19"/48.5 cm long

YARN

▸ Cascade Yarns Cascade 220, (**4**), 100% wool, 220 yds/200 m, 3.5 oz/100 g, 1 skein each Colors 8891 Cyan Blue (A), 9463B Gold (B), 8010 Natural (C), 2409 Palm (D), 8913 Cherry Blossom (E), 9466 Zinnia Red (F)

CROCHET HOOK

▸ US H/8 (5 mm) *or size needed to obtain correct gauge*

GAUGE

▸ 14 sts and 14 rnds = 4"/10 cm in back loop single crochet

OTHER SUPPLIES

▸ Yarn needle

PATTERN ESSENTIALS

BLsc (back loop single crochet)
Work 1 single crochet into the back loop only.

BLsc-dec (back loop single crochet decrease)
Into the 2 stitches indicated, insert hook from front to back through back loop only of first stitch and from back to front through back loop only of 2nd stitch, yarnover and pull up a loop, yarnover and pull through both loops on hook.

standing BLsc (standing back loop single crochet)
Beginning with slip knot on hook, insert hook into back loop only of stitch indicated, yarnover and pull up a loop, yarnover and pull through both loops on hook.

standing sc (standing single crochet)
Beginning with slip knot on hook, insert hook into stitch or space indicated, yarnover and pull up a loop, yarnover and pull through both loops on hook.

working into back bump of chain
With the wrong side of the chain facing, insert hook into the bumps on the back of the chain. (The right side of the chain is a series of Vs.)

• PROJECT NOTES •

▶ Stocking is worked in the round from the top down, with an opening made for the heel. The heel is worked after the foot and toe are complete.

▶ Work leg and foot in 1-rnd stripes of A, B, C, D, E and F. Change to new color on the last slip stitch of the previous round.

Stocking

LEG

► With A, ch 46, join with slip st to form a ring, being careful not to twist chain.

RND 1 (RS): Ch 1, sc in each ch around; with B, join with slip st to back loop of first sc. (46 sc)

RND 2: With B, ch 1, BLsc in each sc around; with C, join with slip st to back loop of first sc.

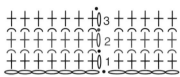

► Continue working 1-round stripes of each color as established, until stocking measures approximately 10"/25 cm from beginning, ending with A. Fasten off.

DIVIDE FOR HEEL: With A, place a slip knot on hook, leaving a 6"/15 cm tail, skip 35 sts, slip st in back loop of next st, ch 23, skip 22 sts, join with slip st in back loop of next st.

► Fasten off, leaving a 6"/15 cm tail.

FOOT

► With B, sc in back bump of 12th ch and in back bump of remaining 11 chs, BLsc in next st (same st as slip st), BLsc in next 22 sc, sc in back loop of each remaining ch; with C, join with slip st to first sc. (46 sts)

► Continuing in established stripe pattern, work even until foot measures approx. 5"/12.5 cm from chain, ending with a rnd of A.

TOE

RND 1: With A, ch 1, BLsc in each sc around, join with slip st to first sc. (46 sc)

RND 2: Ch 1, BLsc in next 2 sc, *BLsc-dec, BLsc in next 2 sc; rep from * around, join with slip st in back loop of first sc. (35 sc)

RNDS 3, 5, 7 AND 9: Ch 1, BLsc in each st around, join with slip st in back loop of first sc.

RND 4: Ch 1, *sc2tog, sc in next 3 sc; rep from * around. (28 sc)

RND 6: Ch 1, *sc in next 2 sc, sc2tog; rep from * around. (21 sc)

RND 8: Ch 1, *sc2tog, sc in next sc; rep from * around. (14 sc)

RND 10: Ch 1, (sc2tog) around. (7 sc)
▸ Fasten off, leaving a 6"/15 cm tail. Thread yarn tail through remaining sts and pull tight to close hole.

HEEL

RND 1: With A and right side facing, standing BLsc in first st of round (at back heel), BLsc in next 10 sc, BLsc-dec in next st and next ch, BLsc in next 21 ch, BLsc-dec in next ch and next sc, BLsc in next 10 sc, join with slip st to first sc. (44 sc)

RND 2: Ch 1, BLsc in each sc around, join with slip st to back loop of first sc.

RND 3: Ch 1, *BLsc in next 2 sc, BLsc-dec; rep from * around, join with slip st to back loop of first sc. (33 sc)

RND 4: Rep Rnd 2.

RND 5: Ch 1, * BLsc-dec, BLsc in next sc; rep from * around, join with slip st to back loop of first sc. (22 sc)

RND 6: Ch 1, (BLsc-dec) around, join with slip st to first sc. (11 sc)

RND 7: Ch 1, sc in next sc, (BLsc-dec) around. (6 sc)
▸ Fasten off, leaving a 6"/15 cm tail. Thread yarn tail through remaining sts and pull tight to close hole.

EDGING

RND 1: With A and RS facing, standing sc in first foundation chain at center back leg, sc in each foundation ch around, join with slip st to first sc. (46 sc)

RND 2: Ch 8, join with a slip st to same stitch, sc in each sc around, join with slip st to first sc.

▸ Fasten off.

FINISHING

▸ Using yarn tails, close gaps at heel corners. Weave in ends.

Peppermint Pinstripes Stocking

SIMPLE CROCHET SEED STITCH is transformed into something special with just a change of color. Using nothing but single crochet and chain stitches, even beginning crocheters can create this charming seamless stocking. Use your favorite worsted-weight yarn and change up the colors to make stockings for the entire family.

FINISHED MEASUREMENTS
- 12"/30.5 cm in circumference, 21"/53.5 cm long

YARN
- Red Heart Soft (4), 100% acrylic, 256 yds/234 m, 5 oz/141 g, 1 skein each Color 9925 Really Red (A), 4601 Off-White (B) and 4420 Guacamole (C)

CROCHET HOOKS
- US I/9 (5.5 mm), *or size needed to obtain gauge*
- US H/8 (5 mm), or one size smaller than hook needed to obtain gauge

GAUGE
- 16 sts and 17 rnds = 4"/10 cm in Seed Stitch with larger hook.

OTHER SUPPLIES
- Stitch marker
- Yarn needle

PATTERN ESSENTIALS

sc2tog (single crochet 2 stitches together)
(Insert hook into next st and pull up
a loop) two times, yarnover and pull
through all 3 loops on hook.

standing sc (standing single crochet)
Beginning with slip knot on hook, insert
hook into stitch or space indicated,
yarnover, pull up a loop, yarnover and
pull through both loops on hook.

• PROJECT NOTES •

▶ Stocking is worked in the
round from the top down,
with an opening made
for the heel. The heel is
worked in rounds without
joining, after the foot and
toe are complete.

▶ Change colors with a slip
stitch at the end of every
round as directed.

SEED STITCH IN THE ROUND

Multiple of 2 sts

Chain an even number, join with slip st in first ch to form a ring, being careful
not to twist chain.

RND 1: Ch 1, working in back bump of each ch around, sc in first ch, *ch 1, skip
1 ch, sc in next ch; rep from * around, omitting last sc; with next color join
with slip st to first sc.

RND 2: Ch 2 (counts as ch-1 space), *skip 1 sc, sc in next space, ch 1; rep from *
around, omitting last ch-1, with next color join with slip st to 2nd ch of ch-2.

RND 3: Ch 1, sc in first space, *ch 1, skip 1 sc, sc in next space; rep from *
around, omitting last sc; with next color join with slip st to first sc.

Rep Rnds 2–3 for pattern.

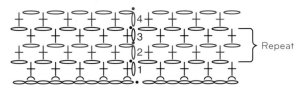

Repeat

SEED STITCH IN THE ROUND

Stocking

LEG

▶ With A and larger hook, ch 48, join with slip st in first ch to form a ring, being careful not to twist chain.

▶ Work Seed Stitch in the Round using one round of each color in the following sequence: A, B, C, A, B, C, A, B, C. Cut C. Working stripes of one round each of A and B only, work even until piece measures 12"/30.5 cm from beginning, ending with a round of B. Do not cut B.

DIVIDE FOR HEEL: With A, work in pattern, ending join with slip st to first ch. Continuing with A, ch 24, skip 24 sts, slip st in next sc. Fasten off, leaving an 8"/20.5 cm tail.

FOOT

▶ With B and larger hook, pull up a loop in same st as slip st; (sc in back bump of next ch, ch 1, skip 1 ch) 12 times, sc in next ch-space (same st as slip st), (ch 1, skip 1 sc, sc in next space) 11 times, ch 1, skip 1 sc; with A, join with slip st to first sc. Work even in stripes of A and B until foot measures 5"/12.5 cm. Cut A and B.

TOE

RND 1: With C and larger hook, work in established pattern. Remainder of Toe is worked in rounds without joining. Place marker in first st of round and move up each round as you work.

RND 2: Ch 1, sc in each sc and ch-1 space around. (48 sc)

RND 3: *Sc in next 2 sc, sc2tog; rep from * around. (36 sc)

RND 4: *Sc in next sc, sc2tog, sc in next sc; rep from * around. (27 sc)

RNDS 5 AND 7: Sc in each sc around.

RND 6: *Sc2tog, sc in next sc; rep from * around. (18 sc)

TOE, *continued*

RND 8: Rep Rnd 6. (12 sc)

RND 9: Sc2tog around. (6 sc)

▸ Fasten off, leaving a 6"/15 cm tail.

HEEL

RND 1: With C and larger hook, standing sc in 7th ch-1 space at back heel, (ch 1, skip 1 sc, sc in next space) five times, skip (sc, space, sc), do not ch 1, sc in next space, (ch 1, skip 1 sc, sc in next space) 10 times, skip (sc, space sc), do not ch 1, sc in next space, (ch 1, skip 1 sc, sc in next space) four times, ch 1, skip 1 sc; *do not join.* (42 sts) Place marker in first st of round and move up each round as you work.

RND 2: Sc in each sc and ch-1 space around.

RND 3: *Sc in next sc, sc2tog; rep from * around. (28 sc)

RND 4: *Sc in next 5 sc, sc2tog; rep from * around. (24 sc)

RND 5: Sc in each sc around.

RND 6: *Sc in next 4 sc, sc2tog; rep from * around. (20 sc)

RND 7: *Sc in next 3 sc, sc2tog; rep from * around. (16 sc)

RND 8: *Sc in next 2 sc, sc2tog; rep from * around. (12 sc)

RND 9: Sc2tog around, slip st in next st. (6 sc)

▸ Fasten off, leaving a 6"/15 cm tail.

EDGING

▸ With A, smaller hook and RS facing, standing sc in space at center back leg, ch 8, sc in each sc and ch-1 space around, join with slip st to first sc. Fasten off.

FINISHING

▸ Using yarn tails, sew holes at toe and heel closed. Close any gaps at corners of heel. Weave in ends.

Flame-Stitch Stocking

YOU GET A BIG DESIGN PUNCH for little work from this Flame-Stitch pattern. It's easy to learn and works up in a snap. To keep colors from twisting, keep the color you are working on to the left [lefties, to the right], and keep the other colors to the right [left]. Use up leftover yarns and play with color combinations — we've shown you two colorways to get you started.

FINISHED MEASUREMENTS

▸ 12½"/32 cm in circumference, 18½"/47 cm long

YARN

▸ Version 1: Brown Sheep Lamb's Pride (4), 85% wool/15% mohair, 190 yds/173 m, 4 oz/113 g, 1 skein each Colors M-06 Deep Charcoal (A), M-03 Grey Heather (B) and M-04 Charcoal Heather (C)

▸ Version 2: Brown Sheep Lamb's Pride (4), 85% wool/15% mohair, 190 yds/173 m, 4 oz/113 g, 1 skein each Color M-38 Lotus Pink (A), Color M-174 Wild Mustard (B) and Color M-22 Autumn Harvest (C)

CROCHET HOOK

▸ US I/9 (5.5 mm) *or size needed to obtain correct gauge*

GAUGE

▸ 14 sts and 12 rnds = 4"/10 cm in Flame Stitch pattern

OTHER SUPPLIES

▸ Stitch marker
▸ Yarn needle

PATTERN ESSENTIALS

sc2tog (single crochet 2 stitches together)
(Insert hook into next st and pull up a loop) two times, yarnover and pull through all 3 loops on hook.

standing dc (standing double crochet)
Beginning with slip knot on hook, yarnover, insert hook into stitch or space indicated, yarnover, pull up a loop, (yarnover and pull through 2 loops on hook) two times.

standing sc (standing single crochet)
Beginning with slip knot on hook, insert hook into stitch or space indicated, yarnover, pull up a loop, yarnover and pull through both loops on hook.

working into back bump of chain
With the wrong side of the chain facing, insert hook into the bumps on the back of the chain. (The right side of the chain is a series of Vs.)

FLAME-STITCH PATTERN

Multiple of 4 sts

RND 1 (RS): Ch 3 (does not count as dc); *dc in next ch-space; working over ch-3, dc in 2nd skipped sc in rnd below, dc in same ch-3 space, ch 1; rep from * around, join with slip st to top of first dc, turn.

RND 2 (WS): Ch 1, sc in next ch-1 space, ch 1, skip 1 dc, sc in next dc, *ch 3, skip (dc, ch 1, dc), sc in next dc; rep from * to last st, ch 1, skip last st; with next color, join with slip st to first sc, turn.

RND 3: With new color, ch 3 (counts as dc), dc in next ch-1 space, *ch 1, dc in next ch-3 space; working over ch-3 and ch-1, dc in skipped sc two rnds below, dc in same ch-3 space of current rnd; rep from * around to last ch-1 space, ch 1, dc in next ch-1 space, join with slip st to top of ch-3, turn.

RND 4: Ch 1, sc in same st, *ch 3, skip (dc, ch 1, dc), sc in next dc; rep from * around, omitting last sc; with next color, join with slip st to first sc, turn.

RND 5: With new color, ch 3 (does not count as dc); *dc in next ch-3 space; working over ch-3 and ch-1, dc in skipped sc two rnds below, dc in same ch-3 space, ch 1; rep from * around, join with slip st to top of first dc, turn.

Rep Rnds 2–5 for pattern.

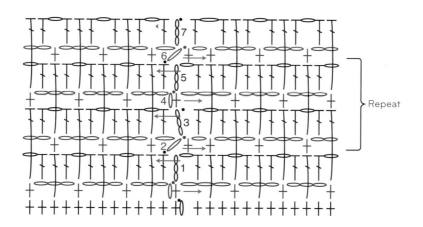

FLAME STITCH

Stocking

LEG

▶ With A, loosely chain 44, join with slip st to form a ring, being careful not to twist chain.

RND 1 (RS): Ch 1, sc in back bump of each ch around, join with slip st to first sc. *Do not turn.* (44 sc)

RND 2: Ch 1, sc in each sc around, join with slip st to first sc, turn.

RND 3 (WS): Ch 1, sc in first sc, ch 3, skip 3 sc, sc in next sc; rep from * around, omitting last sc; with B, join with slip st to first sc, turn. (11 ch-3 spaces)

▶ Beginning with B and RS facing, starting with Rnd 1 of pattern, work Flame Stitch pattern, working 2 rounds each of B, C, and A in sequence, until piece measures approximately 10½"/26.5 cm from beginning, ending with A and Rnd 5 of pattern. *Do not turn at end of last rnd.*

▶ Cut B and C. Fasten off A.

HEEL

ROW 1 (RS): With A, skip first 33 sts and spaces of last rnd; leaving an 8"/20.5 cm tail, standing sc in next dc, sc in next dc, (working over ch-1, dc in next skipped sc in rnd below, sc in next 3 dc) four times, working over ch-1, dc in next skipped sc in rnd below, sc in next 2 dc, turn. (21 sts)

ROW 2 (WS): Ch 1, sc in next 14 sts, turn. (14 sc)

ROW 3: Ch 1, sc in next 7 sc, turn. (7 sc)

ROW 4: Ch 1, sc in next 7 sc, sc in next st of long row below, turn. (8 sc)

ROW 5: Ch 1, sc in next 8 sc, sc in next st of long row below, turn. (9 sc)

ROWS 6–17: Ch 1, sc in each sc across, sc in next st of long row below, turn. (21 sc at end of last row) *Do not turn at end of last row.*

FOOT

RND 1 (RS): Continuing across instep sts, [ch 3, skip (dc, ch 1, dc), sc in next dc] five times, ch 3, skip (dc, ch 1, dc), sc in first sc of heel; continuing across heel sts, (ch 3, skip 3 sc, sc in next sc) five times, slip st in next space. (11 ch-3 spaces) Fasten off A.

RND 2 (RS): With B, skip first 10 sts of heel; working over ch-3, standing dc in next skipped sc in rnd below, (dc in same ch-space, ch 1, dc in next ch-space, working over ch-3, dc in 2nd skipped sc in rnd below) two times, dc in same ch-space, ch 1, dc in next space, (working over ch-3 and ch-1, dc in next skipped sc two rnds below, dc in same ch-space, ch 1, dc in next ch-space) six times, (working over ch-3, dc in 2nd skipped sc in rnd below, dc in same ch-space, ch 1, dc in next space) two times, join with slip st to first dc, turn. (44 sts)

▶ Beginning with Rnd 4 of Flame Stitch Pattern, work even in established pattern until foot measures approximately 5"/12.5 cm from end of heel shaping, ending with C and Rnd 5 of pattern. Join last rnd with A; *do not turn.* Cut B and C.

TOE

RND 1 (RS): With A, ch 1, *sc in next 3 dc; working over ch-1, dc in next skipped sc in the rnd below; rep from * around, join with slip st to first sc, turn.

RND 2: Ch 1, sc in next 10 sc, sc2tog, sc in next 20 sc, sc2tog, sc to end, join with slip st to first sc, turn. (42 sc)

RND 3: Ch 1, *sc in next 5 sc, sc2tog; rep from * around, join with slip st to first sc, turn. (36 sc)

RNDS 4, 6, 8 AND 10 (WS): Ch 1, sc in each sc around, join with slip st to first sc, turn.

RND 5: Ch 1, *sc2tog, sc in next 4 sc; rep from * around, join with slip st to first sc, turn. (30 sc)

RND 7: Ch 1, *sc2tog, sc in next 3 sc; rep from * around, join with slip st to first sc, turn. (24 sc)

RND 9: Ch 1, *sc2tog, sc in next sc; rep from * around, join with slip st to first sc, turn. (16 sc)

TOE, *continued*

RND 11: Ch 1, (sc2tog) around. (8 sc)

▸ Fasten off, leaving a 6"/15 cm tail. Thread tail through remaining sts and pull tight to close hole.

EDGING

▸ Place marker in first foundation chain at back leg. With RS facing and A, working into both remaining loops of foundation ch around top of stocking, work standing sc 1 st to the right of marked st, ch 9, slip st in 2nd ch from hook and next 7 ch; insert hook into free end of piece just made and into marked st, yarnover, pull up a loop, yarnover and pull through all loops on hook (*hanging loop complete*); sc in each foundation ch around, join with slip st to first sc. Fasten off.

FINISHING

▸ Using yarn tails, close gaps at heel corners. Weave in ends.

Snowstorm Stocking

DESIGNED BY BARBARA KREUTER

THE ENCRUSTED, EMBELLISHED LOOK of freeform crochet is well suited to the holidays, when a little excess decoration is called for. This stocking combines a strong, orderly base with a blizzard of appliquéd motifs. Rounds of back loop single crochet present a smooth background on which to highlight the motifs, with a subtle change in the heel and toe to rounds of regular single crochet.

FINISHED MEASUREMENTS

▶ 14"/35.5 cm circumference, 19"/48.5 cm long

CROCHET HOOKS

▶ US E/4 (3.5 mm) *or size needed to obtain correct gauge*
▶ US F/5 (3.75 mm), US G/6 (4 mm), and US H/8 (5 mm) for snowflake motifs

GAUGE

▶ 24 sts and 23 rnds = 4"/10 cm in back loop single crochet
▶ Gauge for snowflake motifs varies and is not critical.

OTHER SUPPLIES

▶ Stitch markers
▶ Yarn needle

YARN

▶ Tahki Yarns Cotton Classic Lite, (3), 100% cotton, 108 yds/100 m, 1.75 oz/50 g, 3 skeins 3003 Linen White (MC)
▶ S. Charles Collezione Crystal, (0), 85% polyester, 15% cotton, 144 yds/131 m, 0.88 oz/25 g, 1 ball 42 Moonlight (A)
▶ S. Charles Collezione Isadora, (4), 75% merino wool, 25% nylon, 125 yds/114 m, 1.75 oz/50 g, 1 ball 01 Pearl (B)
▶ S. Charles Collezione Luna, (0), 71% super kid mohair, 20% silk, 9% lurex, 232 yds/212 m, 0.88 oz/25 g, 1 ball 42 Moonlight (C)
▶ Filatura di Crosa Zarina, (2), 100% superwash merino wool, 181 yds/165 m, 1.75 oz/50 g, 1 ball Color 1396 Off-White (D)

PATTERN ESSENTIALS

BLsc (back loop single crochet)
Work 1 single crochet into the back loop only.

BLsc2tog (back loop single crochet 2 stitches together)
(Insert hook into back loop of next st and pull up a loop) two times, yarnover and pull through all 3 loops on hook.

picot-3
Ch 3, slip st in 3rd ch from hook.

picot-5
Ch 5, slip st in 4th ch from hook.

popcorn
Make 4 dc in one st, remove hook from loop, insert hook from front to back in first dc of group, then into dropped loop, yarnover and draw through both loops on hook.

sc2tog (single crochet 2 stitches together)
(Insert hook into next st and pull up a loop) two times, yarnover and pull through all 3 loops on hook.

sc3tog (single crochet 3 stitches together)
(Insert hook into next st and pull up a loop) three times, yarnover and pull through all 4 loops on hook.

• PROJECT NOTES •

▶ Stocking is worked in rounds without joining beginning with a hanging loop, then working from the cuff down, with shaping at the back of the calf and with an opening made for the heel.

▶ The heel is worked in rounds after the foot and toe are complete.

▶ The snowflake motifs are stitched separately and appliquéd/applied to the stocking in a freeform fashion.

▶ The stitch pattern in the stocking can bias slightly, which makes the beginning of the round move slightly from a true vertical. To check that the beginning of the round is centered on hanging loop, fold the stocking with hanging loop at the fold and move marker to the fold, if necessary.

Stocking

HANGING LOOP

▸ With MC, using hook needed to obtain gauge, begin with adjustable ring.

RND 1: Ch 1, 5 sc in ring; do not join. (5 sc) Place marker in first st of round and move up each round as you work.

RND 2: BLsc in each st around. (5 sts)

▸ Rep Rnd 2 until piece measures 3"/7.5 cm. Do not fasten off.

LEG

▸ Ch 84. Without twisting ch, BLsc in each of last 2 sts of hanging loop cord, place marker in last st made, sc in each ch around. (86 sts) Move marker up each round as you work.

▸ Work even in BLsc until piece measures 5"/12.5 cm. Move marker to center back leg here and throughout calf shaping if necessary (see Project Notes on page 40).

DECREASE ROUND: BLsc in next st, BLsc2tog, BLsc to last 3 sts of rnd, BLsc2tog, BLsc in last st. (84 sts)

▸ Work 5 rnds even.

▸ Rep these 6 rnds four more times. (76 sts at end of last decrease rnd)

▸ Work even in BLsc until piece measures 10½"/26.5 cm.

▸ Move marker to center back leg if necessary.

DIVIDE FOR HEEL: Place markers at 20th and 57th sts from marker; remove marker at center back. BLsc in each st to 1 st before first marker. Fasten off, leaving a 6"/15 cm tail. With MC and slip knot on hook, slip st in back loop of st marked by second marker, ch 38, skip 38 sts, BLsc in next (marked) st, BLsc in next 37 sts, working last BLsc over slip st at beginning of ch. (38 sts)

FOOT

▸ Remove side markers and place marker in 19th ch; sc in each ch to marker. Beginning of rnd is now at center of sole.

RND 1: Sc in each remaining ch, then BLsc in each st around. (76 sts)

▸ Work even in BLsc until foot measures 5"/12.5 cm from chain.

TOE

▸ Move marker to center back leg if necessary. (See Project Notes)

RND 1: Sc in each sc around.

RND 2: *Sc in next 17 sc, sc2tog; rep from * around. (72 sc)

RNDS 3, 5, 6, 8, 9, 11, AND 13: Sc in each sc around.

RND 4: *Sc in next 2 sc, sc2tog, sc in next 2 sc; rep from * around. (60 sc)

RND 7: *Sc in next 3 sc, sc2tog; rep from * around. (48 sc)

RND 10: *Sc in next sc, sc2tog, sc in next sc; rep from * around. (36 sc)

RND 12: *Sc2tog, sc in next sc; rep from * around. (24 sc)

RND 14: *Sc in next sc, sc2tog; rep from * around. (16 sc)

RND 15: Sc2tog around. (8 sc)

▸ Fasten off, leaving a 6"/15 cm tail. Thread tail through last 8 sts, gather tightly to close gap.

HEEL

SET-UP RND: Beginning at right corner of sts on sole side of heel opening, with MC standing sc in first st of opening, sc in next 36 sts across sole, sc2tog (1 st from sole and 1 st from leg), sc in next 36 sts across back of leg, sc2tog (1 st from leg and 1 st from sole), sc in next 18 sts to move beginning of rnd to center of sole. Place marker for beginning of rnd at center of sole.

RND 1: Sc in next 17 sc, sc3tog, sc in next 34 sc, sc3tog, sc in next 17 sc. (70 sc)

RND 2: Sc in next 16 sc, sc3tog, sc in next 32 sc, sc3tog, sc in next 16 sc. (66 sc)

RND 3: Sc in next 15 sc, sc3tog, sc in next 30 sc, sc3tog, sc in next 15 sc. (62 sc)

RND 4: Sc in next 14 sc, sc3tog, sc in next 28 sc, sc3tog, sc in next 14 sc. (58 sc)

RND 5: Sc in next 13 sc, sc3tog, sc in next 26 sc, sc3tog, sc in next 13 sc. (54 sc)

RND 6: Sc in next 10 sc, sc2tog, sc3tog, sc2tog, sc in next 20 sc, sc2tog, sc3tog, sc2tog, sc in next 10 sc. (46 sc)

RND 7: Sc in next 10 sc, sc3tog, sc in next 20 sc, sc3tog, sc in next 10 sc. (42 sc)

RND 8: Sc in next 9 sc, sc3tog, sc in next 18 sc, sc3tog, sc in next 9 sc. (38 sc)

RND 9: Sc in next 6 sc, sc2tog, sc3tog, sc2tog, sc in next 12 sc, sc2tog, sc3tog, sc2tog, sc in next 6 sc. (30 sc)

RND 10: Sc in next 6 sc, sc3tog, sc in next 12 sc, sc3tog, sc in next 6 sc. (26 sc)

RND 11: Sc in next 5 sc, sc3tog, sc in next 10 sc, sc3tog, sc in next 5 sc. (22 sc)

RND 12: Sc in next 2 sc, sc2tog, sc3tog, sc2tog, sc in next 4 sc, sc2tog, sc3tog, sc2tog, sc in next 2 sc. (14 sc)

RND 13: Sc in next 2 sc, sc3tog, sc in next 4 sc, sc3tog, sc in next 2 sc. (10 sc)

▸ Fasten off, leaving a 6"/15 cm tail. Thread tail through last 10 sts, gather tightly to close gap.

Snowflake Motifs

Stitch snowflake motifs separately, varying the yarns used. Make as many motifs as desired; the project shown has a total of 17 motifs. Each of the motif patterns below includes suggestions for yarns and hooks to use in each round, but many other combinations are possible. Do not weave in all ends after working motifs; leave tails that are long enough to use later in stitching motifs to the stocking.

SNOWFLAKE MOTIF No.1

 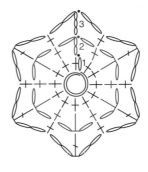

▶ Begin with adjustable ring (see page 171).

RND 1: Ch 1, 12 sc in ring, join with slip st to first sc. (12 sc) Do not tighten adjustable ring.

RND 2: Ch 3 (counts as hdc and ch 1), *sc in next sc, ch 1, hdc in next sc, ch 1; rep from * four times; sc in next sc, ch 1, join with slip st to 2nd ch of ch-3. (12 ch-1 spaces)

RND 3: Ch 5 (counts as dc and ch 2), *sc in next sc, ch 2, dc in hdc, ch 2; rep from * four times; sc in next sc, ch 2, join with slip st to 3rd ch of ch-5. (12 ch-2 spaces) Fasten off. Pull beginning yarn tail to adjust center to the size desired.

Snowflakes shown were worked as follows:

▶ With A and D held together using H/8 (5 mm) hook

▶ With C using F/5 (3.75 mm) hook

SNOWFLAKE MOTIF No.1, continued

▸ With MC using E/4 (3.5 mm) hook

▸ Rnds 1 & 2 with B and Rnd 3 with A and B held together using H/8 (5 mm) hook.

SNOWFLAKE MOTIF No.2

▸ Work as for Snowflake Motif No.1 through Rnd 2.

RND 3: Ch 3 (counts as dc), picot-3, picot-5, picot-3, slip st in top of beginning ch-3, ch 2, *sc in next sc, ch 2, dc in next hdc, picot-3, picot-5, picot-3, slip st in top of dc, ch 2; rep from * four times; sc in next sc, ch 2, join with slip st to top of beginning ch-3. Fasten off. Pull beginning yarn tail to adjust center to the size desired.

Snowflakes shown were worked as follows:

▸ With A and C held together using G/6 (4 mm) hook

▸ With B using H/8 (5 mm) hook

▸ With C using E/4 (3.5 mm) hook

▸ With D using F/5 (3.75 mm) hook

▸ With MC using E/4 (3.5 mm) hook

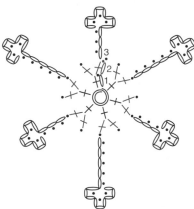

▸ Begin with adjustable ring (see page 171).

RND 1: Ch 1, 6 sc in ring, join with slip st to first sc. (6 sc) Do not tighten adjustable ring.

RND 2: Ch 1, 2 sc in each sc around, join with slip st to first sc. (12 sc)

RND 3: *Ch 3, (picot-3) three times, slip st in each ch of beginning ch-3, slip st in next 2 sc, ch 5, (picot-3) three times, slip st in each ch of ch-5, slip st in next 2 sc; rep from * two times, ending with final slip st in first ch of rnd. Fasten off. Pull beginning yarn tail to adjust center to the size desired.

Snowflakes shown were worked as follows:

▸ With A and C held together using G/6 (4 mm) hook

▸ With A and D held together using H/8 (5 mm) hook

▸ With D using F/5 (3.75 mm) hook

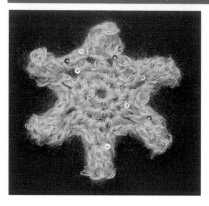

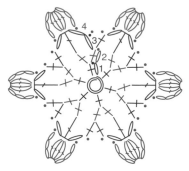

The popcorn edging on this snowflake motif adds dimension. This also makes it more challenging to layer other snowflake motifs over it. On some motifs stitched from this design, omit 1 or 2 adjacent popcorns, substituting simple slip stitches, to make the motif flatter along part of its outer edge. When assembling the stocking, place the popcorn-free section under other motifs.

▸ Begin with adjustable ring (see page 171).

RND 1: Ch 1, sc 6 in ring, join with slip st to first sc. (6 sc) Do not tighten adjustable ring.

RND 2: Ch 1, 2 sc in each sc around, join with slip st to first sc. (12 sc)

RND 3: Ch 2 (counts as sc and ch 1), *dc in next sc, ch 1, 2 sc in next sc, ch 1; rep from * four times, dc in next sc, ch 1, sc in next sc, join with slip st to first ch of rnd.

RND 4: *Slip st in ch-1 space, ch 3, popcorn in dc, ch 3, slip st in ch-1 space, slip st in next 2 sc; rep from * around, join with slip st to first slip st of rnd. Fasten off. Pull beginning yarn tail to adjust center to the size desired.

Snowflakes shown were worked as follows:

- ▸ With A and C held together using F/5 (3.75 mm) hook

- ▸ With D using E/4 (3.5 mm) hook

- ▸ With MC and C held together using G/6 (4 mm) hook

- ▸ Rnds 1–3 with B using H/8 (5 mm) hook; Rnd 4 with MC and A held together using F/5 (3.75 mm) hook

- ▸ Rnds 1–3 with D using E/4 (3.5 mm) hook; Rnd 4 with C using F/5 (3.75 mm) hook

Finishing

BLOCK STOCKING. Position snowflake motifs as desired on stocking, overlapping some snowflakes over others and placing at least one motif to extend over the upper edge of the stocking cuff. Use yarn needle and yarn tails to sew snowflakes to stocking. Sew free end of hanging cord securely to wrong side of stocking to form hanging loop. Weave in ends, using tails at corners of heels to close any gaps.

Creamy Textured Stocking

HERE'S AN ELEGANT STOCKING that will look great in any setting, from a Victorian parlor to a minimalist flat. The naturally colored yarn shows off the stitch pattern nicely. When doing the Trinity Stitch at the foot, take care to match the stitch tension on the leg.

FINISHED MEASUREMENTS

▶ 12"/30.5 cm in circumference, 19"/48.5 cm long

YARN

▶ Universal Yarns Deluxe Worsted (4), 100% Wool, 220 yds/200 m, 3.5 oz/100 g, 2 skeins Color 40001 Cream Natural

CROCHET HOOK

▶ US H/8 (5.0 mm) *or size needed to obtain correct gauge*

GAUGE

▶ 16 stitches and 16 rnds = 4"/10 cm in single crochet

▶ 16 stitches and 13½ rnds = 4"/10 cm in Trinity Stitch

OTHER SUPPLIES

▶ Stitch marker
▶ Yarn needle

• PROJECT NOTES •

▶ Stocking is worked in the round from the top down. Each round is joined, then turned to work alternate rounds in opposite directions. The heel is worked using short rows.

PATTERN ESSENTIALS

picot-3
Ch 3, slip st in 3rd ch from hook.

sc2tog (single crochet 2 stitches together)
(Insert hook in next st and pull up a loop) two times, yarn-over and pull through all 3 loops on hook.

sc cluster (single crochet cluster)
Insert hook into same st and pull up a loop, (insert hook into next st or space and pull up a loop) two times, yarnover and pull through all 4 loops on hook.

standing sc (standing single crochet)
Beginning with slip knot on hook, insert hook into stitch indicated, yarn-over, pull up a loop, yarnover and pull through both loops on hook.

working into back bump of chain
With the wrong side of the chain facing, insert hook into the bumps on the back of the chain. (The right side of the chain is a series of Vs.)

TRINITY STITCH

Multiple of 2 + 1

RND 1: Ch 1, sc in same st, *sc cluster, ch 1; rep from * around, join with slip st to first sc, turn.

RND 2: Ch 1, sc in first sc, sc cluster pulling up loops in (same st as sc, next ch-space, and top of next cluster), ch 1, *sc cluster pulling up loops in (same place as third leg of previous cluster, next ch-space, and top of next cluster), ch 1; rep from * around, join with slip st to first sc, turn.

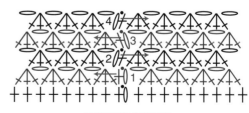

TRINITY STITCH

Rep Rnd 2 for pattern.

Stocking

CUFF AND LEG

FOUNDATION CH: Ch 50, join with slip st to form a ring, being careful not to twist chain.

RND 1 (RS): Ch 1, sc in back bump of each ch around, join with slip st to first sc. Mark this side as right side, turn. (50 sc)

RNDS 2–3: Ch 1, sc in each sc around, join with slip st to first sc, turn.

RND 4: Ch 5, skip 4 sc, slip st in next sc; rep from * around, turn.

RND 5: Ch 1, (sc, hdc, dc, picot-3, dc, hdc, sc) in each ch-space around, join with slip st to first sc, turn.

RND 6: Ch 3 (counts as dc), dc in each sc of Row 3 around (including the same sts as the slip sts from Rnd 4), join with slip st to first dc, turn.

RND 7: Ch 1, sc in each dc around, join with slip st to first sc, turn.

RNDS 8–14: Rep Rnds 4–7 once, then Rnds 4–6 once.

RND 15: Ch 1, sc2tog, sc in each sc around. Do not turn. (49 sc)

▶ Beginning with Rnd 1 of Trinity Stitch, work even in Trinity Stitch until stocking measures 10½"/26.5 cm from beginning, ending with a WS row.

▶ Fasten off.

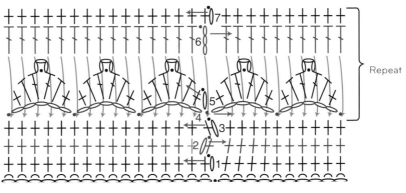

CUFF

HEEL

ROW 1 (RS): Skip first 37 sts, standing sc in next st, sc in next 24 sts, turn. (25 sts)

ROW 2 (WS): Ch 1, sc in first 17 sc, turn.

ROW 3: Ch 1, sc in first 9 sc, turn.

ROW 4: Ch 1, sc in first 9 sc, sc in next st of rnd below, turn. (10 sc)

ROW 5: Ch 1, sc in first 10 sc, sc in next st of rnd row below, turn. (11 sc)

RNDS 6–19: Ch 1, sc in each sc across, sc in next st of rnd row below, turn. (25 sc at end of last row)

▸ Fasten off, leaving an 8"/20.5 cm tail.

FOOT

RND 1 (RS): Skip first 12 sc of heel, standing sc in next st, continue in Trinity St across heel sts and instep stitches.

▸ Work even in established stitch pattern on 49 sts until foot measures 5"/12.5 cm from end of heel shaping, ending with RS row.

TOE

RNDS 1, 3, 5, 7 AND 9 (WS): Ch 1, sc in each sc around, join with slip st to first sc, turn.

RND 2: Ch 1, *sc in next 5 sc, sc2tog; rep from * around, join with slip st to first sc, turn. (42 sc)

RND 4: Ch 1, *sc2tog, sc in next 4 sc; rep from * around, join with slip st to first sc, turn. (35 sc)

RND 6: Ch 1, *sc in next 3 sc, sc2tog; rep from * around, join with slip st to first sc, turn. (28 sc)

RND 8: Ch 1, *sc2tog, sc in next 2 sc; rep from * around, join with slip st to first sc, turn. (21 sc)

RND 10: Ch 1, sc in next sc, (sc2tog) around, join with slip st to first sc, turn. (11 sc)

RND 11: Rep Rnd 10. (6 sc)

▸ Fasten off. Thread tail through sts and pull tight to close hole.

EDGING

▶ Place marker in first foundation ch at back of leg. With RS facing, working into both remaining loops of foundation ch around top of stocking, work standing sc 1 st to the right of marked st, ch 9, slip st in 2nd ch from hook and next 7 ch; insert hook into free end of piece just made and into marked st, yo, pull up a loop, yo and pull through all loops on hook (*hanging loop complete*); sc in each foundation ch around, join with slip st to first sc. Fasten off.

FINISHING

▶ Using yarn tails, close gaps at heel corners. Weave in ends.

Basketweave Stocking

A RUSTIC YARN AND TEXTURED STITCH PATTERN evoke Christmas in a cozy mountain cabin with a roaring fire in the hearth. Use a solid or heathered color to show up the stitch pattern. Front post and back post stitches create the classic basketweave, while short rows form the heel.

FINISHED MEASUREMENTS

- 13½"/34.5 cm in circumference, 18½"/47 cm long

YARN

- Imperial Yarn Columbia (4), 100% wool, 220 yds/200 m, 4 oz/113 g, 2 skeins Color 66 Cocoa Heather

CROCHET HOOK

- US I/9 (5.5 mm) *or size needed to obtain correct gauge*

GAUGE

- 12 sts and 10 rnds = 4"/10 cm in Basketweave Stitch

OTHER SUPPLIES

- Stitch marker
- Yarn needle

PATTERN ESSENTIALS

BPdc (back post double crochet)
Yarnover, insert hook from back to front to back around post of next stitch
and pull up a loop, (yarnover and pull through two loops on hook) two
times.

FPdc (front post double crochet)
Yarnover, insert hook from front to back to front around post of stitch indicated and pull up a loop, (yarnover and pull through two loops on hook)
two times.

sc2tog (single crochet 2 stitches together)
(Insert hook into next st and pull up a loop) two times, yarnover and pull
through all 3 loops on hook.

standing sc (standing single crochet)
Beginning with slip knot on hook, insert hook into stitch indicated, yarnover, pull up a loop, yarnover and pull through both loops on hook.

working into back bump of chain
With the wrong side of the chain
facing, insert hook into the bumps
on the back of the chain. (The right
side of the chain is a series of Vs.)

● **PROJECT NOTE** ●

▶ Stocking is worked in the
round from the top down. Each
round is joined, then turned
to work alternate rounds in
opposite directions.

BASKETWEAVE STITCH

Multiple of 6 sts

SET-UP RND 1 (WS): Ch 3 (counts as dc), dc in each sc around, join with slip st to top of ch-3, turn.

SET-UP RND 2: Ch 2 (does not count as dc here and throughout), *FPdc in next 3 dc, BPdc in next 3 dc; rep from * around, join with slip st to first FPdc, turn.

RND 1: Ch 2, *FPdc in next 3 sts, BPdc in next 3 sts; rep from * to last st, join with slip st to first FPdc, turn.

RNDS 2–3: Ch 2, *BPdc in next 3 sts, FPdc in next 3 sts; rep from * to last st, join with slip st to first BPdc, turn.

RND 4: Rep Row 1.

Rep Rnds 1–4 for pattern.

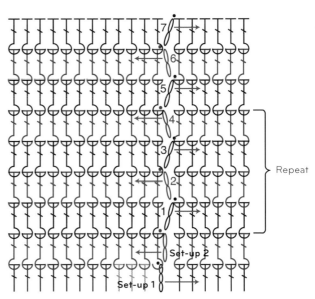

BASKETWEAVE STITCH

Stocking

LEG

▸ Loosely chain 42, join with slip st to form a ring, being careful not to twist chain.

RND 1 (RS): Ch 1, sc in each back bump of each ch around, join with slip st to first sc. *Do not turn.* (42 sc)

RND 2: Ch 1, sc in each sc around, join with slip st to first sc, turn.

▸ With WS facing, beginning with Set-up Rnd 1, work in Basketweave Stitch until piece measures approximately 10½"/26.5 cm from beginning, ending with Rnd 1 of pattern.

▸ Fasten off.

HEEL

ROW 1 (RS): With right side facing, skip first 33 sts of last rnd, leaving an 8"/20.5 cm tail, standing sc in next sc, sc in next 20 sc, turn, leaving remaining sts unworked. (21 sc)

ROW 2 (WS): Ch 1, sc in next 14 sc, turn. (14 sc)

ROW 3: Ch 1, sc in next 7 sc, turn. (7 sc)

ROW 4: Ch 1, sc in next 7 sc, sc in next st of long row below, turn. (8 sc)

ROW 5: Ch 1, sc in next 8 sc, sc in next st of long row below, turn. (9 sc)

ROWS 6–17: Ch 1, sc in each sc across, sc in next st of long row below, turn. (21 sc at end of last row)

▸ Fasten off, leaving an 8"/20.5 cm tail.

FOOT

RND 1 (RS): Skip first 9 sc of heel, work standing dc in next sc, dc in next 11 heel sc; working across stocking instep, (BPdc in next 3 sts, FPdc in next 3 sts) three times, BPdc in next 3 sts; working across heel sts, dc in next 9 sc, join with slip st to first dc, turn. (42 sts)

▸ Beginning with Rnd 3 of Basketweave Pattern, work even until foot measures approximately 7"/18 cm, ending with Rnd 2 of pattern.

RNDS 1, 3, 5, 7 AND 9 (WS): Ch 1, sc in each sc around, join with slip st to first sc, turn.

RND 2: Ch 1, *sc in next 5 sc, sc2tog; rep from * around, join with slip st to first sc, turn. (36 sc)

RND 4: Ch 1, *sc2tog, sc in next 4 sc; rep from * around, join with slip st to first sc, turn. (30 sc)

RND 6: Ch 1, sc in next sc, *sc2tog, sc in next 3 sc; rep from * around, join with slip st to first sc, turn. (24 sc)

RND 8: Ch 1, *sc2tog, sc in next sc; rep from * around, join with slip st to first sc, turn. (16 sc)

RND 10: Ch 1, (sc2tog) around, join with slip st to first st. (8 sc)

RND 11: Rep Rnd 10. (4 sc)

▸ Fasten off. Thread tail through sts and pull tight to close hole.

EDGING

▸ Place marker in first foundation ch at back leg. With RS facing, working into both remaining loops of foundation ch around top of stocking, work standing sc 1 st to the right of marked st, ch 9, slip st in 2nd ch from hook and next 7 ch; insert hook into free end of piece just made and into marked st, yo, pull up a loop, yo and pull through all loops on hook (*hanging loop complete*); sc in each foundation ch around, join with slip st to first sc. Fasten off.

FINISHING

▸ Using yarn tails, close gaps at heel corners. Weave in ends.

Ripple-Stitch Stocking

UNEXPECTED COLORS AND A CLASSIC RIPPLE STITCH combine in this nontraditional stocking. Surface crochet stripes highlight the ripple pattern. Unusual heel construction creates additional dimension while maintaining the zigzags in leg and foot. Hint: You may prefer to work the surface crochet stripes as you crochet, rather than just before working the heel.

FINISHED MEASUREMENTS

▶ 12½"/32 cm in circumference, 20"/51 cm long, measured from top peak to toe

YARN

▶ Cascade Yarns Cascade 220 (4), 100% Peruvian Highland Wool, 220 yds/200 m, 3.5 oz/100 g, 1 skein each Colors 8891 Cyan Blue (A), 9430 Highland Green (B), 7818 Blue Velvet (C), 9463B Gold (D)

CROCHET HOOKS

▶ US I/9 (5.5 mm) *or size needed to obtain correct gauge*
▶ US H/8 (5 mm) *or one size smaller than size needed to obtain correct gauge*

GAUGE

▶ One 16-st pattern repeat = 3"/7.5 cm in Ripple Stitch
▶ 12 rnds = 4"/10 cm in Ripple Stitch

OTHER SUPPLIES

▶ Stitch marker
▶ Yarn needle

PATTERN ESSENTIALS

sc3tog (single crochet 3 stitches together)
(Insert hook into next st and pull up a loop) three times, yarnover and pull through all 4 loops on hook.

sc5tog (single crochet 5 stitches together)
(Insert hook into next st and pull up a loop) five times, yarnover and pull through all 6 loops on hook.

standing sc (standing single crochet)
Beginning with slip knot on hook, insert hook into stitch or space indicated, yarnover, pull up a loop, yarnover and pull through both loops on hook.

surface chain
Holding yarn on wrong side of fabric, insert hook from front to back into next st and pull up a loop through fabric and through loop on hook.

working into back bump of chain
With the wrong side of the chain facing, insert hook into the bumps on the back of the chain. (The right side of the chain is a series of Vs.)

PROJECT NOTES

▶ Stocking is worked in the round from the top down, with an opening made for the heel. The heel is worked in three sections, after the foot and toe are complete.

▶ For best results, do not carry the colors loosely up the wrong side, but cut them on each color change. Change colors on the last stitch of a round by using the new color to complete the joining slip stitch.

RIPPLE STITCH PATTERN

Multiple of 16 sts

RND 1: Ch 1, 2 sc in same ch, *sc in next 6 ch, sc3tog, sc in next 6 ch**, 3 sc in next ch; rep from * around, ending last rep at **, sc in beg ch, join with slip st to first sc.

RND 2: Ch 1, 2 sc in same st, *sc in next 6 sc, sc3tog, sc in next 6 sc**, 3 sc in next sc; rep from * around, ending last rep at **, sc in same st as first st of rnd, join with slip st to first sc.

Rep Rnd 2 for pattern.

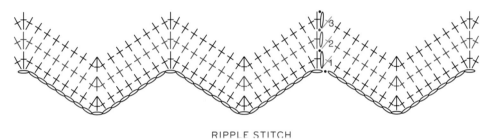

RIPPLE STITCH

STRIPE SEQUENCE

RNDS 1 AND 2: A

RND 3: B

RND 4: C

RNDS 5 AND 6: A

RNDS 7 AND 8: C

RNDS 9–11: B

RND 12: C

Rep Rnds 1–12 for Stripe Sequence.

Stocking

LEG

FOUNDATION CH: With A and larger hook, ch 64, join with slip st to form a ring, being careful not to twist chain.

▸ Working in Ripple Stitch pattern, beginning with Rnd 1, work Rnds 1–12 of the Stripe Sequence two times, then Rnds 1–5 once more, ending with 1 rnd of A.

DIVIDING FOR THE HEEL: With A, ch 33, skip (1 valley, 1 peak, 1 valley), slip st in center st of next peak. Fasten off.

FOOT

▸ With A and larger hook, standing sc in center of skipped peak, sc in same st, sc in next 6 sc, sc3tog, sc in next 6 sc; (working in back bumps of chain, 3 sc in next ch, sc in next 6 ch, sc3tog over next 3 ch, sc in next 6 ch) two times, 3 sc in back bump of next ch, sc in next 6 sc, sc3tog, sc in next 6 sc, sc in same st as first st of rnd, join with slip st to first sc. (64 sts)

▸ Continuing in established Ripple Stitch and Stripe Sequence, work Rnds 7–12 once, then Rnds 1–12 once, ending with 1 rnd of A; *do not fasten off*. Cut B and C.

▸ Foot length from chain measures approximately 6"/15 cm measured from the top of a peak to the corresponding valley.

TOE

RND 1: With A, ch 1, 2 sc in same st, *sc in next 5 sc, sc5tog, sc in next 5 sc**, 3 sc in next sc; rep from * around, ending last rep at **, sc in same st as first st of rnd, join with slip st to first sc. (56 sc)

RND 2: Ch 1, 2 sc in same st, *sc in next 4 sc, sc5tog, sc in next 4 sc**, 3 sc in next sc; rep from * around, ending last rep at **, sc in same st as first st of rnd, join with slip st to first sc. (48 sc)

RND 3: Ch 1, 2 sc in same st, *sc in next 3 sc, sc5tog, sc in next 3 sc**, 3 sc in next sc; rep from * around, ending last rep at **, sc in same st as first st of rnd, join with slip st to first sc. (40 sc)

RND 4: Ch 1, 2 sc in same st, *sc in next 2 sc, sc5tog, sc in next 2 sc**, 3 sc in next sc; rep from * around, ending last rep at **, sc in same st as first st of rnd, join with slip st to first sc. (32 sc)

RND 5: Ch 1, 2 sc in same st, *sc in next sc, sc5tog, sc in next sc**, 3 sc in next sc; rep from * around, ending last rep at **, sc in same st as first st of rnd, join with slip st to first sc. (24 sc)

RND 6: Ch 1, sc in same st, *sc5tog, sc in next sc; rep from * around, omitting last sc, sc in same st as first st of rnd, join with slip st to first sc. (8 sc)

▸ Fasten off, leaving a 6"/15 cm tail. Thread yarn tail through remaining sts and pull tight to close hole.

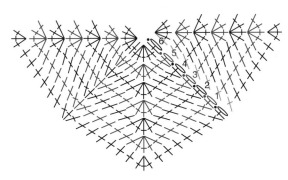

TOE PATTERN

EMBELLISHMENT

▸ Beginning at back of heel with smaller hook and D, work surface chain around the circumference of the stocking, in the center of all Color A stripes. Use photo as a guide and take care to work all surface chains in the same direction.

HEEL

SECTION 1

RND 1: With A, ch 4 loosely; with RS facing and toe pointing down, sc in center sc at right peak on bottom of foot, sc in next 6 ch, sc3tog, sc in next 7 ch, ch 4 loosely, join with sl st to first ch. (23 sts: 8 ch and 15 sc)

RND 2: Ch 1, sc in back bump of next 3 ch; insert hook in back bump of next ch, yo and pull up a loop, skip 1 sc, insert hook in next sc, yo and pull up a loop, yo and pull through all 3 loops on hook to sc2tog; sc in next 4 sc, sc3tog, sc in next 4 sc; insert hook in next sc, yo and pull up a loop, skip 1 sc, insert hook in back bump of next ch, yo and pull up a loop, yo and pull through all 3 loops on hook to sc2tog, sc in back bump of last 3 ch, join with slip st to first sc. (17 sts)

RND 3: Ch 1, sc in next 2 st, (sc3tog, sc in next 2 sts) three times, join with slip st to first sc. (11 sts)

RND 4: Ch 1, sc in next sc, (sc3tog) three times, sc in next sc; do not join. (5 sts)

▸ Fasten off, leaving a 6"/15 cm tail. Thread yarn through remaining sts and pull tight to close.

SECTION 2

▸ Place one marker in foot 1 st to the left of Section 1; place a second marker in foot 1 st to the right of Section 1.

RND 1: With RS facing and A, standing sc in marked st to the right of Section 1, sc in next 4 foundation ch of Section 1; working along leg sts, sc in center sc at peak of center back leg chevron, (sc in next 6 sc, sc3tog) two times, sc in next 5 sc, join with slip st to first sc. (25 st)

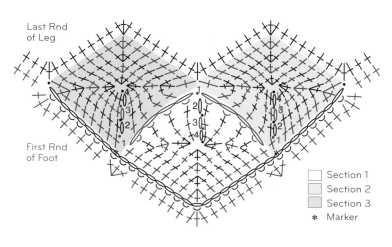

Last Rnd of Leg

First Rnd of Foot

☐ Section 1
☐ Section 2
▦ Section 3
✳ Marker

HEEL PATTERN

RND 2: Ch 1, sc in next 4 sc, (sc3tog, sc in next 4 sc) three times, join with slip st to first sc. (19 sts)

RND 3: Ch 1, sc in next 3 sc, (sc3tog, sc in next 2 sc) three times, sc in last sc, join with slip st to first sc. (13 sts)

RND 4: Ch 1, sc in next 2 sc, (sc3tog) three times, sc in last 2 sc; do not join. (7 sts)
- Fasten off, leaving a 6"/15 cm tail. Thread yarn through remaining sts and pull tight to close.

SECTION 3

RND 1: With RS facing and A, standing sc in marked st to the left of Section 1, sc in next 5 sc, sc3tog over next 2 ch and next st on last rnd of leg; working along leg sts, sc in next 6 sc, sc3tog, sc in next 7 sc (including same center sc at Section 2 corner), sc in next 4 foundation ch, join with slip st to first sc. (25 sts)

RND 2: Ch 1, sc in next 5 sc, (sc3tog, sc in next 4 sc) three times, omitting last sc, join with slip st to first sc. (19 sts)

RND 3: Ch 1, sc in next 4 sc, (sc3tog, sc in next 2 sc) three times, join with slip st to first sc. (13 sts)

RND 4: Ch 1, sc in next 3 sc, (sc3tog) three times, sc in last sc, join with slip st to first sc; do not join. (7 sts)
- Fasten off, leaving a 6"/15 cm tail. Thread yarn through remaining sts and pull tight.

EDGING
- With A and RS facing, standing sc at upper back valley of stocking, ch 8, sc in same st; work in Ripple Stitch pattern around, join with slip st to first sc. Fasten off, leaving a 6"/15 cm tail.

FINISHING
- Use yarn tails at heel corners and sections to close any existing gaps. Weave in ends.

Candy Cane Stocking

DESIGNED BY CAROL VENTURA

INTERMEDIATE AND ADVANCED CROCHETERS will delight in this retro-look striped stocking. Cotton yarn worked using tapestry crochet techniques makes a sturdy fabric to hold plenty of goodies (for information about tapestry crochet, see page 73). Personalize the stocking using the alphabet charts provided. If you've never tried tapestry crochet, this is a perfect project to learn on, with instructions given for both right- and left-handed crocheters. Take time to read the instructions and notes both before and during the stitching.

FINISHED MEASUREMENTS

▸ 14½"/37 cm in circumference at top, 24"/61 cm long

YARN

▸ Classic Elite Provence (2), 100% mercerized cotton, 102 yds/93 m, 1.75 oz/50 g, 4 skeins Color 5827 French Red (A), 3 skeins Color 5816 Natural (B)

CROCHET HOOK

▸ US E/4 (3.5 mm) *or size needed to obtain correct gauge*

▸ A hook with a handle is recommended for doing tapestry crochet.

GAUGE

▸ 25 sts and 22 rows = 4"/10 cm in tapestry crochet

OTHER SUPPLIES

▸ Stitch marker

▸ Yarn needle

PATTERN ESSENTIALS

sc2tog (single crochet 2 stitches together)
(Insert hook into next st and pull up a loop) two times, yarnover and pull through all 3 loops on hook.

• PROJECT NOTES •

▶ The toe, foot, leg, and cuff are worked in rounds without joining. The heel is crocheted back and forth in rows using one of the right-side facing techniques (see opposite page).

▶ Change colors when two loops remain on the hook; yarnover with the next color and pull it through both loops to complete the stitch.

▶ Single crochet stitches slant to the right when crocheted with the right hand and to the left when crocheted with the left hand. The toe and leg of the pictured project were crocheted in rounds with the right hand. The same instructions work for left-handed crocheters, although the stripes will slant in the opposite direction. Instructions are given for both right- and left-handed crocheters; where the instructions differ each will be written separately.

▶ After Round 2, throughout the entire stocking one color yarn is single crocheted, while the other color is carried (see opposite page).

TAPESTRY CROCHET

Tapestry crochet is a multicolor crochet technique that uses tightly worked single crochet stitches to create a sturdy fabric with no yarn floats to snag on the wrong side of the fabric.

The yarn not in use is carried. To carry a yarn, lay the yarn over the top of the stitches being worked into, then single crochet across as usual, encasing the carried yarn. If done correctly, the carried yarn will be only slightly visible from the front and back of the work.

Because the right side of the single crochet stitch — the smoother side — is always facing the right side of the fabric, tapestry crochet is most often worked in the round. However, it is possible to achieve a similar effect when working back and forth in rows, using one of the following methods:

> **DO NOT TURN AT THE END OF THE FIRST ROW,** but switch hands and work with your nondominant hand, single crocheting in the other direction. In other words, right-handed crocheters would work every other row from left to right (i.e., left-handed), and vice versa.

OR

> **TURN THE WORK AS USUAL,** but insert the hook *from back to front* as you work each single crochet stitch across (as shown below).

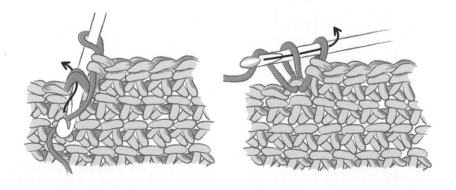

Stocking

TOE AND FOOT

▸ With A, ch 4, join with slip st to form a ring.

RND 1: 6 sc in ring, carrying tail under sts. (6 sc) Place a marker in the first st of the rnd and move it up as you work the rnds.

RND 2: Pull on the yarn tail to make the ring smaller; 2 sc in each sc around. (12 sc)

RND 3: Cut A tail flush. Begin carrying B throughout rnd. With A, 2 sc in each sc around. (24 sc)

RND 4: (With B, 2 sc in next sc; with A, sc in next sc, 2 sc in next sc, sc in next sc) six times. (36 sc)

RND 5: (With B, sc in next sc, 2 sc in next sc; with A, sc in next 2 sc, 2 sc in next sc, sc in next sc) six times. (48 sc)

RND 6: (With B, sc in next sc, 2 sc in next sc, sc in next sc; with A, sc in next 5 sc) six times. (54 sc)

RND 7: (With B, sc in next 4 sc; with A, sc in next 2 sc, 2 sc in next sc, sc in next 2 sc) six times. (60 sc)

RNDS 8–11: (With B, sc in next 4 sc; with A, sc in next 6 sc) six times.

RND 12: (With B, sc in next 4 sc; with A, sc in next 3 sc, 2 sc in next sc, sc in next 2 sc) six times. (66 sc)

RNDS 13–14: (With B, sc in next 4 sc; with A, sc in next 7 sc) six times.

RND 15: (With B, sc in next 4 sc; with A, sc in next 3 sc, 2 sc in next sc, sc in next 3 sc) six times. (72 sc)

RNDS 16–47: (With B, sc in next 4 sc; with A, sc in next 8 sc) six times. Remove marker.

▸ See charts on page 77.

For right-handed crocheters only

▸ Do not cut yarn.

ROW 48: Using one of the right-side facing techniques described on page 73 to work from left to right, skip first st; with A, sc in next 6 sc, (with B, sc in next 4 sc; with A, sc in next 8 sc) twice; with B, sc in next 4 sc; with A, sc in next 4 sc, sc2tog, sc in next 3 sc, (with B, sc in next 4 sc; with A, sc in next 8 sc) twice; with B, sc in next 3 sc, leave last st unworked. (69 sc)

For left-handed crocheters only

RND 48: Continuing from left to right; with B, sc in next 3 sc, (with A, sc in next sc, sc2tog, sc in next sc) twice, (with B, sc in next 4 sc; with A, sc in next 8 sc) twice; with B, sc in next 4 sc; with A, sc in next 4 sc, sc2tog, sc in next 3 sc, (with B, sc in next 4 sc; with A, sc in next 8 sc) twice; with B, sc in next 3 sc. The last 3 B sts are over the first 3 B sts. (69 sc)

For both right- and left-handed crocheters

ROW 49: Crocheting right to left, skip first st; with B, sc in next sc, (with A, sc in next 8 sc; with B, sc in next 4 sc) three times; with A, sc in next 4 sc, sc2tog, sc in next 3 sc; with B, sc in next 4 sc; with A, sc in next 8 sc; with B, sc in next 4 sc; with A, sc in next 5 sc. (66 sc)

ROW 50: Crocheting left to right, skip first st; with A, sc in next 3 sc, (with B, sc in next 4 sc; with A, sc in next 8 sc) twice; with B, sc in next 4 sc; with A, sc in next 4 sc, sc2tog, sc in next 3 sc, (with B, sc in next 4 sc; with A, sc in next 8 sc) twice. (63 sc)

ROW 51: Crocheting right to left, skip first st; with A, sc in next 6 sc, (with B, sc in next 4 sc; with A, sc in next 8 sc) twice; with B, sc in next 4 sc; with A, sc in next 4 sc, sc2tog, sc in next 3 sc; with B, sc in next 4 sc; with A, sc in next 8 sc; with B, sc in next 4 sc; with A, sc in next 2 sc. (60 sc)

ROW 52: Crocheting left to right, skip first st; with B, sc in next 4 sc, (with A, sc in next 8 sc; with B, sc in next 4 sc) twice; with A, sc in next 4 sc, sc2tog, sc in next 3 sc; with B, sc in next 4 sc; with A, sc in next 8 sc; with B, sc in next 4 sc; with A, sc in next 5 sc. (57 sc)

ROW 53: Crocheting right to left, skip first st; with A, sc in next 3 sc, (with B, sc in next 4 sc; with A, sc in next 8 sc) twice; with B, sc in next 4 sc; with A, sc in next 4 sc, sc2tog, sc in next 3 sc; with B, sc in next 4 sc; with A, sc in next 8 sc; with B, sc in next 3 sc. (54 sc)

ROW 54: Crocheting left to right, skip first st; with B, sc in next sc, (with A, sc in next 8 sc; with B, sc in next 4 sc) twice; with A, sc in next 4 sc, sc2tog, sc in next 3 sc; with B, sc in next 4 sc; with A, sc in next 8 sc; with B, sc in next 4 sc; with A, sc in next 2 sc. (51 sc)

ROW 55: Crocheting right to left, skip first st, (with B, sc in next 4 sc; with A, sc in next 8 sc) twice; with B, sc in next 4 sc; with A, sc in next 4 sc, sc2tog, sc in next 3 sc; with B, sc in next 4 sc; with A, sc in next 8 sc. (48 sc)

ROW 56: Crocheting left to right, skip first st; with A, sc in next 6 sc; with B, sc in next 4 sc; with A, sc in next 8 sc; with B, sc in next 4 sc; with A, sc in next 4 sc, sc2tog, sc in next 3 sc; with B, sc in next 4 sc; with A, sc in next 8 sc; with B, sc in next 3 sc. (45 sc)

ROW 57: Crocheting right to left, skip first st; with B, sc in next sc, (with A, sc in next 8 sc; with B, sc in next 4 sc) twice; with A, sc in next 4 sc, sc2tog, sc in next 3 sc; with B, sc in next 4 sc; with A, sc in next 5 sc. (42 sc)

ROW 58: Crocheting left to right, skip first st; with A, sc in next 3 sc; with B, sc in next 4 sc; with A, sc in next 8 sc; with B, sc in next 4 sc; with A, sc in next 4 sc, sc2tog, sc in next 3 sc; with B, sc in next 4 sc; with A, sc in next 8 sc. (39 sc)

ROW 59: Crocheting right to left, skip first st; with A, sc in next 6 sc; with B, sc in next 4 sc; with A, sc in next 8 sc; with B, sc in next 4 sc; with A, sc in next 4 sc, sc2tog, sc in next 3 sc; with B, sc in next 4 sc; with A, sc in next 2 sc. (36 sc)

ROW 60: Crocheting left to right, skip first st; with B, sc in next 4 sc; with A, sc in next 8 sc; with B, sc in next 4 sc; with A, sc in next 4 sc, sc2tog, sc in next 3 sc; with B, sc in next 4 sc; with A, sc in next 5 sc. (33 sc)

ROW 61: Crocheting right to left, skip first st; with A, sc in next 3 sc; with B, sc in next 4 sc; with A, sc in next 8 sc; with B, sc in next 4 sc; with A, sc in next 4 sc, sc2tog, sc in next 3 sc; with B, sc in next 3 sc. (30 sc)

ROW 62: Crocheting left to right, skip first st; with B, sc in next sc; with A, sc in next 8 sc; with B, sc in next 4 sc; with A, sc in next 4 sc, sc2tog, sc in next 3 sc; with B, sc in next 4 sc; with A, sc in next 2 sc. (27 sc)

ROW 63: Crocheting right to left, skip first st; with B, sc in next 4 sc; with A, sc in next 8 sc; with B, sc in next 4 sc; with A, sc in next 4 sc, sc2tog, sc in next 3 sc. (24 sc)

ROW 64: Crocheting left to right, skip first st; with A, sc in next 6 sc; with B, sc in next 4 sc; with A, sc in next 4 sc, sc2tog, sc in next 3 sc; with B, sc in next 3 sc. (21 sc)

For right-handed crocheters only:

ROW 65: Crocheting right to left, skip first st; with B, sc in next sc; with A, sc in next 8 sc; with B, sc in next 4 sc; with A, sc in next 7 sc. (20 sc)

For left-handed crocheters only:

ROW 65: Skip this row and proceed to Rnd 66 for left-handed crocheters.

HEEL STITCH CHARTS

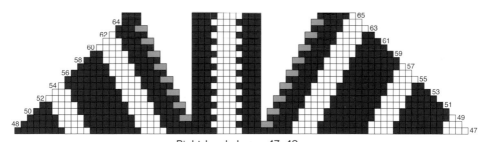

Right-handed, rows 47–49
Right- and Left-handed, Rows 50–65

Rows 47–49 (Left-Handed)

Chart Key
■ sc in A
□ sc in B
▨ Sc2tog in A

LEG

For right-handed crocheters only:

RND 66: Working into the edges of the rows for part of the round, working A sts evenly over A sections and B sts evenly over B sections, with A, sc in next st, (with B, sc in next 4 sts; with A, sc in next 8 sts) six times. (72 sts; the last A sc is crocheted into the first A st of this rnd). Place a marker in the first st of the rnd and move it up as you work the rnds.

For left-handed crocheters only:

RND 66: (Note: There is no Rnd 65) Working from left to right into the edges of the rows for part of the rnd, working A sts evenly over A sections and B sts evenly over B sections, with B sc in next st; with A, sc in next 8 sts, (with B, sc in next 4 sts; with A, sc in next 8 sts) five times. (72 sts) Place a marker in the first st of the rnd and move it up as you work the rnds.

For both right- and left-handed crocheters:

RNDS 67 AND 68: (With B, sc in next 4 sc; with A, sc in next 8 sc) six times. (72 sc)

RND 69: (With B, sc in next 4 sc; with A, sc in next 4 sc, 2 sc in next sc, sc in next 3 sc) six times. (78 sc)

RNDS 70–88: (With B, sc in next 4 sc; with A, sc in next 9 sc) six times.

RND 89: (With B, sc in next 4 sc; with A, sc in next 4 sc, 2 sc in next sc, sc in next 4 sc) six times. (84 sc)

RNDS 90–108: (With B, sc in next 4 sc; with A, sc in next 10 sc) six times.

RND 109: (With B, sc in next 4 sc; with A, sc in next 5 sc, 2 sc in next sc, sc in next 4 sc) six times. (90 sc)

RNDS 110–129: (With B, sc in next 4 sc; with A, sc in next 11 sc) six times.

RNDS 130–132: Carrying A throughout, with B, sc in each sc around.

- Use the "Dad" chart provided, or make your own. (See box below.)

- Each square on the chart represents 1 single crochet. The letters do not begin in the center of the panel, but they will become centered as you work additional rounds.

PERSONALIZING THE STOCKING

Referring to the alphabet chart on page 81, choose letters or initials that will fit into the 37-square-wide blank chart provided. Using a pencil, draw the letters in the rectangle, centering them as much as possible.

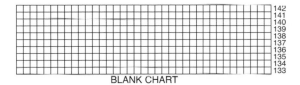

BLANK CHART

For right-handed crocheters only:

RND 133: (With B, sc in next 7 sc; with A and B, work chart across next 37 sc; with B, sc in next sc) twice.

For left-handed crocheters only:

RND 133: (With B, sc in next 8 sc; with A and B, work chart across next 37 sc; with B, sc in next 37 sc) twice.

LETTERS, continued

For both right-handed and left-handed crocheters:

RNDS 134–142: Work in pattern as established.

RND 143: Continuing to carry A throughout, with B, sc in next 3 sc, ch 30 to form hanging loop, sc in each sc around. (120 sc)

RND 144: Continuing to carry A throughout, with B, sc in next 3 sc, sc in each of next 30 ch, sc in each sc around.

RND 145: Continuing to carry A throughout, with B, sc in each sc around, cut A flush with work, slip st in next st.

▶ Fasten off.

FINISHING

▶ End B is not woven in but threaded on a needle and embedded in stitches with the carried color.

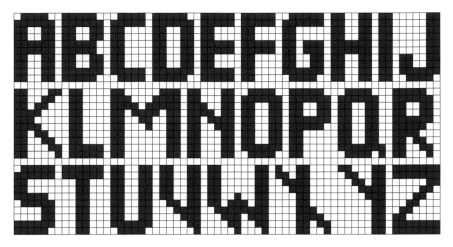

RIGHT-HANDED

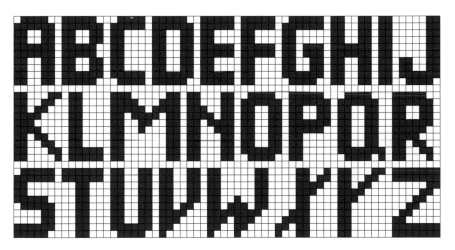

LEFT-HANDED

Chart Key
■ sc in A
□ sc in B

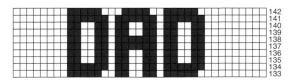

For the Tree

Felted Ornaments

USE UP YOUR SMALL AMOUNTS of non-superwash wool yarn for these easy and fun-to-do ornaments. The felting takes care of uneven stitches, but you can leave them unfelted if you prefer. We've shown you a few samples here; once you get started you can probably think of dozens of ways to put these techniques to use. Even the kids can get into the act — it's a perfect family project! For advice on how to felt, see page 177.

FINISHED MEASUREMENTS

▶ 2–3" (5–7.5 cm) diameter, felted

YARN

▶ Cascade Yarns Cascade 220, (4), 100% wool, 220 yds/200 m, 3.5 oz/100 g, small amounts each Colors 8891 Cyan Blue (A), 9463B Gold (B), 8010 Natural (C), 2409 Palm (D), 8913 Cherry Blossom (E), 9466 Zinnia Red (F), 7825 Orange Sherbet (G)

CROCHET HOOK

▶ Size J/10 (6 mm) *or size needed to obtain correct gauge*

GAUGE

▶ Large Circle = 3"/7.5 cm diameter, before felting

OTHER SUPPLIES

▶ Yarn needle
▶ Two ¾" buttons (JHB #45140 Peoria in Green)
▶ Sewing needle and red thread
▶ Monofilament for hanging

• PROJECT NOTES •

▶ Simple-as-can-be hand-sewing techniques are all you need to complete the ornaments.

▶ If not using the yarn specified, choose a non-superwash 100% wool yarn to ensure that it felts.

PATTERN ESSENTIALS

BLdc (back loop double crochet)
Work 1 double crochet into the back loop only.

FLdc (front loop double crochet)
Work 1 double crochet into the front loop only.

picot-3
Ch 3, slip st in 3rd ch from hook.

standing BLdc (standing back loop double crochet)
Beginning with slip knot on hook, yarnover, insert hook into back loop only of stitch indicated, yarnover, pull up a loop, (yarnover and pull through 2 loops on hook) two times.

standing sc (standing single crochet)
Beginning with slip knot on hook, insert hook into stitch or space indicated, yarnover, pull up a loop, yarnover and pull through both loops on hook.

LARGE CIRCLE

Ch 4, join with slip st to form a ring.

RND 1 (RS): Ch 3 (counts as dc), 15 dc in ring, join with slip st to top of ch-3. (16 dc)

RND 2: Ch 3 (counts as dc), dc in same st, *2 dc in next 2 dc, dc in next dc; rep from * around, join with slip st to top of ch-3. (27 dc)

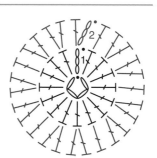

Fasten off. Weave in ends.

MEDIUM CIRCLE

Ch 4, join with slip st to form a ring.

RND 1 (RS): Ch 3 (counts as dc), 15 dc in ring, join with slip st to top of ch-3. (16 dc)

RND 2: Ch 1, sc in same st, 2 sc in next dc, *sc in next dc, 2 sc in next dc; rep from * around, join with slip st to top of ch-3. (18 sc)

Fasten off. Weave in ends.

SMALL CIRCLE

Make as for Large Circle through Rnd 1.

Fasten off. Weave in ends.

Ornament №1

Make 1 Medium Circle each in A, B, D, and G. Felt the circles.

▸ **HANGING LOOP:** Cut three 60"/1.5 m strands of E and work twisted cord (see page 178) approx. 22"/56 cm long. Insert unknotted end of twisted cord through center of one circle; leaving a 4"/10 cm tail of cord at bottom of circle, tie a loose overhand knot and snug it up next to circle to form spacer knot; *insert unknotted end of cord through center of next circle, tie spacer knot next to circle; rep from * for each remaining circle, omitting knot after last circle. Thread unknotted end of cord back down through center hole of all four circles. Adjust parallel ends of cord to leave an approximately 3"/7.5 cm loop at top of ornament. Tie doubled cord into an overhand knot near bottom circle. Cut both cords and unwind strands back to knot to form tassel.

Ornament №2

Make 2 Small Circles in B. Make 2 Medium Circles in F. Make 1 Large Circle in D. Felt the circles.

▸ Stack circles from small to large to small as shown in photo. Cut three 36"/91 cm strands of B and work twisted cord approximately 12"/30.5 cm long. Thread unknotted end of cord up through center of circles, then back down. Adjust parallel ends of cord to leave an approximately 2½"/6.5 cm loop at top of ornament. Tie doubled cord into an overhand knot near bottom circle. Cut both cords and unwind strands back to knot to form tassel.

Ornament №3

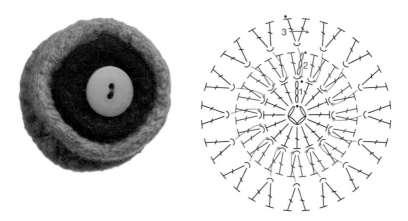

With D, ch 4, join with slip st to form a ring.

RND 1 (RS): Ch 3 (counts as dc), 15 dc in ring, join with slip st to front loop at top of ch-3 (16 dc)

RND 2: Ch 3 (counts as dc), FLdc in same st, (2 FLdc) in each dc around, join with slip st to top of ch-3. (32 dc) Fasten off.

RND 3: With WS facing and working into free loops of Rnd-1 sts, standing FLdc in any Rnd-1 stitch, FLdc in same dc, 2 FLdc in each dc around. (32 dc)

▸ Fasten off. Weave in ends.

▸ Make 2 Small Circles in F. Felt the circles, allowing edges of larger circle to cup outward.

▸ Stack 1 Small Circle and one ¾"/2 cm button on each side of cupped circle. With sewing needle and thread, sew in place. Hang with monofilament threaded through center of assembled circles.

Ornament №4

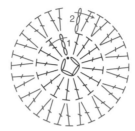

FIRST CIRCLE

▸ With F, ch 4, join with slip st to form a ring.

ROW 1 (RS): Ch 3 (counts as dc), 15 dc in ring; do not join, turn. (16 dc)

ROW 2 (WS): Ch 3 (counts as dc), dc in same st, 2 dc in each st across; do not join. (32 dc)

▸ Leaving a 5"/12.5 cm tail, do not fasten off in the ordinary way, but cut yarn and pull tail through last stitch.

SECOND CIRCLE

▸ With C, ch 4 loosely; slip tail of chain into beginning ring of first circle, join with slip st to form a ring. The beginning chain-rings of the two circles are now intertwined.

▸ Work Rows 1 and 2 as for first circle.

▸ Thread yarn tail of first circle onto yarn needle. Insert needle under V of 16th dc of second circle, around 3rd ch of ch-3 of first circle, back under same dc of second circle, then back from top to bottom into last st of first circle to complete an invisible tapestry needle join (at right). Repeat invisible tapestry needle join to close second circle under 16th st of first circle. Weave in ends. Felt ornament. Hang with monofilament.

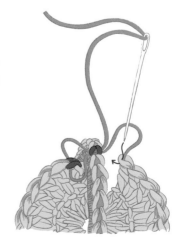

Ornament №5

 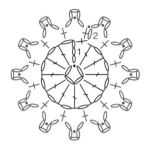

With F, ch 4, join with slip st to form a ring.

RND 1: Ch 4 (counts as dc and ch 1), (dc, ch 1) 10 times in ring, dc in ring, join with sc to 3rd ch of ch-4.

RND 2: Ch 1, sc in space formed by joining ch, *ch 1, picot-3, ch 1, sc in next space; rep from * around, omitting last sc, join with slip st to first sc.

▸ Fasten off and weave in ends. Felt the circle.

▸ Cut a 40"/1 m length of D. With yarn needle and leaving a 3"/7.5 cm tail on right side, thread D from right side to wrong side through center hole, over edge of ornament between two picots, and back through center hole; continue in this manner to wrap yarn around outside edge of ornament between each picot. When twelve wraps are complete, yarn tails will be on opposite sides. Thread yarn under a couple of wraps on wrong side, then back through center hole to right side. Tie ends in bow and trim ends. Hang with monofilament.

Ornament №6

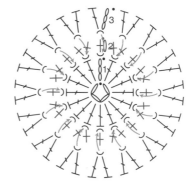

With C, ch 4, join with slip st to form a ring.

RND 1 (RS): Ch 3 (counts as dc), 15 dc in ring, join with slip st to top of ch-3. (16 dc)

RND 2: Ch 1, FLsc in same st, 2 FLsc in next dc, *FLsc in next dc, 2 FLsc in next dc; rep from * around, join with slip st to first sc. (24 sc) Fasten off.

RND 3: With F and working in Rnd-1 sts, standing BLdc in any st, BLdc in same st, 2 BLdc in each st around. (32 dc)

▸ Fasten off. Weave in ends.

▸ Make a second circle, leaving a 12"/30.5 cm yarn tail for sewing. Hold circles with wrong sides together. With MC, sew circles together using a running stitch (at right) just below the Vs at the top of the outer stitches.

▸ Felt the circles. Hang with monofilament.

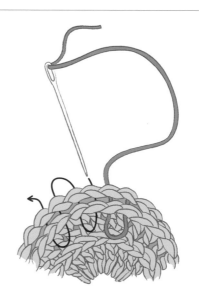

Beaded Garland

THE SIMPLEST OF STITCH PATTERNS turns into a surprisingly beautiful garland when worked in a metallic yarn with bead embellishments. Once the beads are strung, you'll find this a portable and lightweight project. To make it even easier, omit the beads and just rely on the sparkly yarn for your glitz, or use a yarn with prestrung beads.

FINISHED MEASUREMENTS

► 1½"/4 cm wide, 4½ yds/4 m long

YARN

► Lion Brand Vanna's Glamour (2), 96% acrylic/4% metallic polyester, 202 yds/185 m, 1.75 oz/50 g, 1 ball Color 171 gold

CROCHET HOOK

► US F/5 (3.75 mm) *or size needed to obtain correct gauge*

GAUGE

► 8 rows in pattern = 4"/10 cm long

OTHER SUPPLIES

► 876 (about 22 g) size 8 glass beads (Gold AB Miyuki Seed Beads from Caravan Beads)

► Bead needle or sewing thread threader, sewing thread for beads

Garland

String 876 beads onto yarn. (See glossary, page 177.) Chain 4.

ROW 1: Slide 3 beads up to hook, 7 dc in 4th ch from hook, turn.

ROW 2: Ch 3 (does not count as dc), slide 3 beads up to hook, 7 dc in same st, turn. (7 dc)

► Rep Row 2 for desired length. (Sample shown with 292 repeats total.)

► Fasten off and weave in ends.

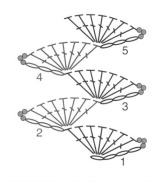

Angel Ornaments

DESIGNED BY KRISTIN OMDAHL

EACH OF THESE ADORABLE ANGELS can be whipped up in only a few minutes. You could decorate your tree with a dozen in one afternoon! The yarn's wispy texture conjures the image of angels appearing out of the clouds. You can make 12 to 14 angels from these two balls of yarn (held together throughout). A whole choir of angels awaits!

FINISHED MEASUREMENTS

▶ Large Angel: 5¼"/13.5 cm wide x 4¼"/11 cm tall

▶ Small Angel: 4½"/11.5 cm wide x 4"/10 cm tall

YARN

▶ Filatura di Crosa Nirvana (1), 100% extrafine superwash merino wool, 375 yds/343 m, .88 oz/25 g, 1 ball Color 01 White (A),

▶ Filatura di Crosa Superior (2), 70% cashmere/25% silk/15% extrafine merino, 330 yds/300 m, .88 oz/25 g. 1 ball color 01 White (B)

CROCHET HOOK

▶ US G/6 (4 mm) *or size needed to obtain correct gauge*

GAUGE

▶ With A and B held together as one, 24 dc = 4"/10 cm

▶ Gauge is not critical for this project *(but see note, page 9).*

PATTERN ESSENTIALS

3dtr-cl (3 double treble cluster)
[(Yarnover) three times, insert hook into stitch indicated and pull up a loop, (yarnover, pull through two loops on hook) three times] three times, yarnover and pull through all four loops on hook.

4dtr-cl (4 double treble cluster)
[(Yarnover) three times, insert hook into stitch indicated and pull up a loop, (yarnover, pull through two loops on hook) three times] four times, yarnover and pull through all five loops on hook.

picot-3
Ch 3, slip st in 3rd ch from hook.

• PROJECT NOTES •

▶ Because they are worked in one piece, there's no finishing needed.

▶ Yarns A and B are held together throughout.

TIP: If using a substitute yarn for the project, choose one that is lightweight and airy so the angels' skirts hang correctly.

Large Angel

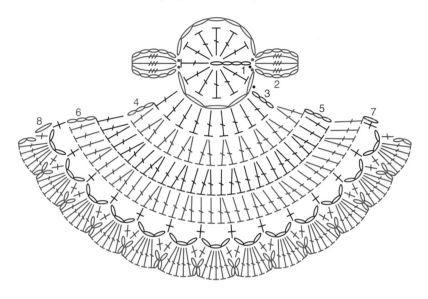

RND 1: Ch 4 (ch 3 counts as first dc), 11 dc in 4th ch from hook, join with slip st to top of 3rd ch at beg of round. (12 dc)

RND 2: Ch 5, 3dtr-cl in first st, ch 5, slip st in same st, ch 7, skip 5 sts, slip st in next st, ch 5, 3dtr-cl in same st, ch 5, slip st in same st, ch 5, skip last 5 sts, join with slip st in first st at beg of rnd, turn.

ROW 3: Slip st in ch-5 space, ch 3 (counts as dc), 9 dc in same space, turn. (10 dc)

ROW 4: Ch 3 (counts as dc), dc in same st, 2 dc in each dc across, turn. (20 dc)

ROW 5: Ch 3 (counts as dc), dc in same st, dc in next dc, *2 dc in next dc, dc in next dc; rep from * across, turn. (30 dc)

ROW 6: Ch 3 (counts as dc), dc in same st, dc in next 2 dc, *2 dc in next dc, dc in next 2 dc; rep from * across, turn. (40 dc)

ROW 7: Ch 1, sc in same st, *ch 3, skip 2 dc, sc in next dc; rep from * across, turn. (13 ch-3 spaces)

ROW 8: Ch 1, (sc, ch 2, 5 dc, ch 2, sc) in each ch-5 space across. (13 5-dc scallops)

▸ Fasten off. Weave in ends.

Small Angel

RND 1: Ch 4 (ch 3 counts as first dc), 11 dc in 4th ch from hook, join with slip st to top of 3rd ch at beg of round. (12 dc)

RND 2: Ch 4, 4dtr-cl in first st, picot-3, ch 4, slip st in same st, ch 4, picot-3, ch 4, skip 5 sts, slip st in next st, ch 4, 4dtr-cl in same st, picot-3, ch 4, slip st in same st at base of cluster, ch 5, skip last 5 sts, join with slip st first st at beg of rnd, turn.

ROW 3: Slip st in ch-5 space, ch 3 (counts as dc), 8 dc in same ch-5 space, turn. (9 dc)

ROW 4: Ch 1, sc in same st, ch 3, skip 2 sts, sc in space before next st, ch 3, skip 3 sts, sc in space before next st, ch 3, skip 2 sts, sc in last st, turn. (3 ch-3 spaces)

ROW 5: Slip st in first ch-3 space, ch 3 (counts as dc), 5 dc in same ch-3 space, 6 dc in each ch-3 space across, turn. (18 dc)

ROW 6: Ch 1, sc in same st, ch 3, skip 2 sts, sc in space before next st, *ch 3, skip 3 sts, sc in space before next st; rep from * to last 3 sts, ch 3, skip 2 sts, sc in last st, turn. (6 ch-3 spaces)

ROW 7: Slip st in first ch-3 space, ch 3 (counts as dc), 5 dc in same sp, 6 dc in each ch-3 space across, turn. (36 dc)

ROW 8: Ch 1, sc in same st, ch 3, skip 2 sts, sc in space before next st, *ch 3, skip 3 sts, sc in space before next st; rep from * to last 3 sts, ch 3, skip 2 sts, sc in last st, turn. (12 ch-3 spaces)

ROW 9: (Sc, ch 3, sc) two times in each space across. (24 ch-3 spaces)

▸ Fasten off. Weave in ends.

Bird Trio

DESIGNED BY ANDEE GRAVES

DECORATE YOUR HOME OR TREE with these beautiful little birds, a traditional symbol of hope and renewal that is perfect for celebrating the season. Best of all, you can crochet up a whole flock of little birds in an afternoon.

FINISHED MEASUREMENTS

▸ 3"/7.5 cm tall

YARN

▸ Universal Yarn Deluxe Worsted, (4), 100% wool, 220 yds/200 m, 3.75 oz/106 g, 1 skein each Color 12294 Real Red (A), Color 91868 Vivid Blue (B), Color 40001 Cream Natural (C)

▸ Each bird takes approximately 33 yds/30 m.

CROCHET HOOK

▸ US F/5 (3.75 mm) *or size needed to obtain correct gauge*

GAUGE

▸ 4 rnds sc = 1½"/4 cm in diameter

▸ *Gauge is not crucial in this project; fabric should be consistent and tight.*

OTHER SUPPLIES

▸ Stitch markers

▸ Yarn needle

▸ Solid Black 6 mm Safety Eyes (samples used Darice Eyes)

▸ Polyester fiber stuffing

▸ 1"/2.5 cm square of yellow craft felt for each bird

▸ Sewing needle and thread to match craft felt

PATTERN ESSENTIALS

sc2tog (single crochet 2 stitches together)
(Insert hook into next st and pull up a loop) two times,
yarnover and pull through all 3 loops on hook.

sc3tog (single crochet 3 stitches together)
(Insert hook into next st and pull up a loop) three times,
yarnover and pull through all 4 loops on hook.

working into back bump of chain
With the wrong side of the chain facing, insert hook into the bumps on the back of the chain. (The right side of the chain is a series of Vs.)

• PROJECT NOTES •

▶ The birds are made in pieces and sewn together. Head, Breast, and Wings are fastened off with 15"/38 cm long tails to use for sewing together.

▶ All pieces are sewn together using a whipstitch. Body, Breast, and Head are sewn together by using the top two loops of each outside stitch.

Bird

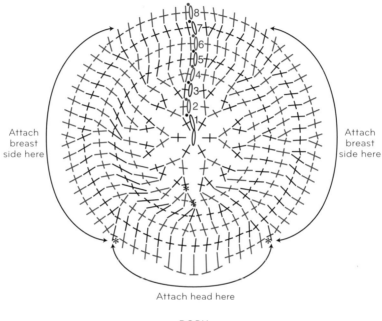

Attach breast side here

Attach breast side here

Attach head here

BODY

RND 1 (RS): Ch 2, 6 sc in 2nd ch from hook, join with slip st to first sc. (6 sc)

RND 2: Ch 1, 2 sc in each sc around, join with slip st to first sc. (12 sc)

RND 3: Ch 1, 2 sc in each sc around, join with slip st to first sc. (24 sc)

RND 4: Place marker in 12th st from join, ch 1, 2 sc in next 2 sc, *(sc next 3 sc, 2 sc next st) two times**, 2 sc next sc, 3 sc in marked sc (place marker in 3rd sc), 2 sc next 2 sc; rep from * to ** once, 2 sc in next sc, sc next st, join with slip st to first sc. (36 sc)

RND 5: Ch 1, (sc next 4 sc, 2 sc next sc) three times, sc next sc, 2 sc next sc, sc next sc, 3 sc in marked sc (remove marker), (sc next sc, 2 sc next sc) two times, (sc next 4 sc, 2 sc next sc) two times, sc next 2 sc, 2 sc next sc, join with slip st to first sc. (47 sc)

BODY, *continued*

RND 6: Ch 1, (sc next 5 sc, 2 sc next sc) seven times, sc next 5 sc, join with slip st to first sc. (54 sc)

RND 7: Ch 1, (sc next 6 sc, 2 sc next sc) three times, sc in next 11 sc, (2 sc next sc, sc next 6 sc) three times, 2 sc in next st, slip st to first sc of round. (61 sc)

RND 8: Ch 1, (sc next 7 sc, 2 sc next sc) three times, sc next 4 sc, hdc next 5 sc, sc next 4 sc, (2 sc next sc, sc next 7 sc) three times, join with slip st to first sc. (62 sc, 5 hdc)

▶ Fasten off. Place marker in 27th and 41st st.

HEAD

RND 1: Ch 2, 6 sc in 2nd ch from hook, join with slip st to first sc. (6 sc)

RND 2: Ch 1, 2 sc each sc, join with slip st to first sc. (12 sc)

RND 3: Ch 1, (sc next 3 sc, 2 sc next sc) three times, join with slip st to first sc. (15 sc)

▶ Fasten off, leaving a long tail for sewing.

HEAD

BREAST

ROW 1: Ch 2, sc in 2nd ch from hook, turn. (1 sc)

ROW 2: Ch 1, 3 sc in sc, turn. (3 sc)

ROW 3: Ch 1, sc in first sc, 2 sc next sc, sc next sc, turn. (4 sc)

ROW 4: Ch 1, 2 sc in first st, sc next 2 sc, 2 sc next sc, turn. (6 sc)

ROW 5: Ch 1, sc in next 6 sc, turn.

ROW 6: Repeat Row 5.

ROW 7: Ch 1, sc in next 2 sc, 2 sc in next 2 sc, sc in next 2 sc, turn. (8 sc)

ROW 8: Ch 1, sc in next 8 sc, turn.

ROWS 9–11: Repeat Row 8 three times.

ROW 12: Ch 1, sc in next 2 sc, (sc2tog) twice, sc in next 2 sc, turn. (6 sc)

ROWS 13 AND 14: Repeat Row 5 two times.

ROW 15: Ch 1, sc2tog, sc next 2 sc, sc2tog, turn. (4 sc)

ROW 16: Ch 1, sc in first st, sc2tog, sc next st, turn. (3 sc)

ROW 17: Ch 1, sc3tog, turn. (1 st)

ROW 18: Ch 1, sc in next st.

EDGING: Ch 1, turn 90 degrees to work along side, sc in side of next 6 rows, 2 sc in side of next row, sc in side of next 4 rows, 2 sc in side of next row, sc in side of next 5 rows, 3 sc in bottom of Row 1; turn to work along other side, starting with Row 2 sc in sides of next 5 rows, 2 sc in next row, sc in sides of next 4 rows, 2 sc in next row, sc in next 6 rows, slip st in top of next st. (41 sc)

▶ Fasten off, leaving a long tail for sewing.

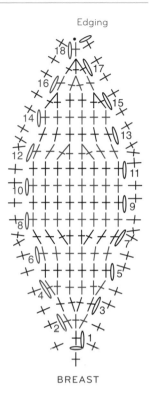

Edging

BREAST

WING (MAKE 2)

▶ Wings are worked in continuous rounds. Place marker at the first stitch of the round and move it up as you work the rounds.

RND 1: Ch 2, 6 sc in 2nd ch from hook. (6 sc)

RND 2: 2 sc in next 6 sc. (12 sc)

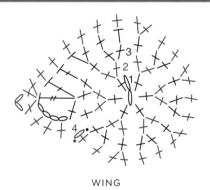

WING

WING, *continued*

RND 3: (2 sc in next sc, sc in next sc) six times, then continuing part way around to finish rnd, hdc next sc, sc next sc, (sc, hdc) in next sc, dc in next st, (dc, tr, ch 4, sc) in next st, skip next st, slip st in next st. (21 sc, 2 hdc, 2 dc, 1 tr)

RND 4: Ch 1, sc in same st, sc in next st, (2 sc in next st, sc in next 2 sc) four times, sc in next 4 sc, (2 sc, ch 2, sc) in next st, skip 1 ch, sc in next 3 ch, slip st in first sc of rnd. (28 sc)

▸ Fasten off, leaving a long tail for sewing.

FINISHING

▸ Weave in beginning tails on all pieces.

▸ Sew Head to Body along sts 27–41 using ending tail; *do not fasten off.*

▸ Place Breast with ending tail at base of Head wrong sides together to Body. Using remaining tail from Head and starting with same st as last st on Head, sew Breast to Body along one side of Breast. (21 sts) Weave in rest of tail from Head. *Tip: On first st of Breast, sew through both st on Head and st on Body.*

▸ Insert safety eyes between 2 sc on either side of hdcs. Fill head with stuffing.

▸ Using ending tail from Breast, sew opposite side of Breast to Body starting at Head (21 sts). Do not cut tail.

▸ Stuff Body firmly through opening at tail. Fold tail flat, making sure all stuffing is in Body cavity. Use remaining Breast tail to sew a running stitch along base of tail to center round of Body to close opening. Weave in remaining ends.

▸ Place Wings along sides and sew in place, stitching around rounded end.

BEAK

▸ Cut Beak shape from craft felt.

▸ Referring to diagram, fold point B to point C. Starting at point A, whip stitch to close raw edges to points B and C. Then place Beak on bird's Head. Weave in ends.

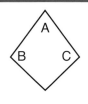

BEAK

Modern Tree Skirt

ADD SOME CONTEMPORARY COLOR to your Christmas décor with this dimensional stitch pattern. The stitching is easier than it looks. The skirt will lie flat or drape nicely, as shown in the photo. It's also easy to make the skirt larger to fit the size of your tree: Just continue in pattern to increase 24 stitches every three rounds.

FINISHED MEASUREMENTS

▸ 36"/91 cm in diameter

YARN

▸ Berroco Vintage (4), 52% acrylic/40% wool/8% nylon, 217 yds/198 m, 3.5 oz/100 g, 5 skeins Color 51103 Clary (MC), 2 skeins 5167 Dewberry (A), 1 skein 5123 Blush (B)

CROCHET HOOK

▸ Size J/10 (6 mm) or size needed to obtain correct gauge

GAUGE

▸ 12 sts = 4"/10 cm in Railing Stitch
▸ 9 rows = 3½"/9 cm in Railing Stitch
▸ See instructions for gauge swatch below.

OTHER SUPPLIES

▸ Yarn needle
▸ Stitch marker (optional)

PATTERN ESSENTIALS

FPtr (front post treble crochet)
(Yarnover) two times, insert hook from front to back to front around post of stitch indicated and pull up a loop (yarnover and pull through two loops on hook) three times.

RAILING STITCH

With MC, ch 19.

ROW 1 (RS): Dc in 4th ch from hook and in each ch across, turn. (17 dc)

ROW 2 (WS): Ch 3 (counts as dc here and throughout), dc in each dc across, turn.

(continued on page 112)

NOTE: On Rows 4, 7, and 10, stitches are worked through double thickness of the last two rows.

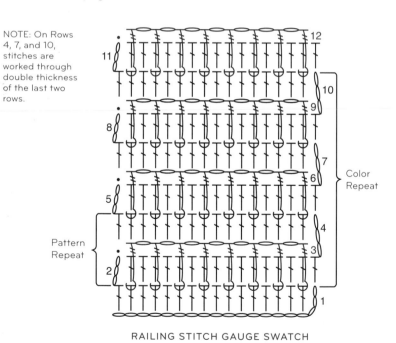

RAILING STITCH GAUGE SWATCH

RAILING STITCH, *continued*

ROW 3 (RS): Drop MC loop and place on stitch marker if desired; draw up a loop of A in same st; with A, FPtr around post of next st 2 rows below, *ch 1, skip 1 st, FPtr around post of next st 2 rows below; rep from * across, ending slip st in top of turning ch of last row. Fasten off contrasting color. *Do not turn.*

ROW 4 (RS, JOINING ROW):
(See Joining Row below.) Replace MC st onto hook, ch 3 (counts as dc), dc in each st and ch-1 space to last st, dc in last st, turn.

Rep (Rows 2–4) three times. Fasten off. *Note: Color sequence will vary.*

● PROJECT NOTES ●

▶ Skirt is worked back and forth in rows from the center out.

▶ The pattern instructions "in next st" means "in next st or space" as described below.

JOINING ROW

Contrasting color rows are worked into the row below the previous row. The following row, in the background color, joins the top of the contrasting color stitches to the background. When working these joining rows, work through double thickness of last 2 rows, by inserting the hook through both the stitch or space of the contrasting color row and the corresponding background stitch in the preceding row, to join the pair of stitches.

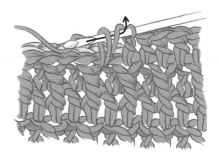

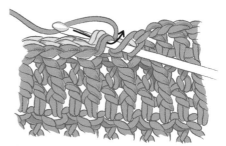

Tree Skirt

With MC, chain 49.

ROW 1 (RS): Dc in 4th ch from hook and in each ch across, turn. (47 dc)

ROW 2 (WS): Ch 3 (counts as dc here and throughout), dc in each dc across, turn.

ROW 3 (RS): Drop MC loop and place on stitch marker if desired; draw up a loop of A in same st; with A, FPtr around post of next st 2 rows below, *ch 1, skip 1 st, FPtr around post of next st in row below previous row; rep from * across, ending slip st in top of turning ch of previous row. Fasten off contrasting color. *Do not turn.*

ROW 4 (RS, INCREASE/JOINING ROW): Replace MC st on hook, ch 3, working through double thickness of the last 2 rows (see Joining Row on facing page), *2 dc in next st, dc in next st; rep from * to last 2 sts, 2 dc in next 2 sts, turn. (71 sts)

ROWS 5 AND 6: Rep Rows 2 and 3.

ROW 7 (RS, INCREASE/JOINING ROW): Replace MC st on hook, ch 3, dc in same st, *2 dc in next st, dc in next 2 sts; rep from * to last st, dc in last st, turn. (95 sts)

ROW 8: Rep Row 2.

ROW 9: With B, rep Row 3.

ROW 10 (RS, INCREASE/JOINING ROW): Replace MC st on hook, ch 3, *2 dc in next st, dc in 3 sts; rep from * to last 2 sts, 2 dc in next st, dc in last st, turn. (119 sts)

ROWS 11 AND 12: Rep Rows 2 and 3.

ROW 13 (RS, INCREASE/JOINING ROW): Replace MC st on hook, ch 3, *dc in next 2 sts, 2 dc in next st, dc in next 2 sts; rep from * to last 3 sts, dc in next st, 2 dc in next st, dc in last st, turn. (143 sts)

ROW 14 AND 15: Rep Rows 2 and 3.

ROW 16 (RS, INCREASE/JOINING ROW): Replace MC st on hook, ch 3, dc in same st, *2 dc in next st, dc in next 5 sts; rep from * to last 4 sts, dc in last 4 sts, turn. (167 sts)

ROW 17: Rep Row 2.

ROW 18: With B, rep Row 3.

ROW 19 (RS, INCREASE/JOINING ROW): Replace MC st on hook, ch 3, *2 dc in next st, dc in next 6 sts; rep from * to last 5 sts, 2 dc in next st, dc in last 4 sts, turn. (191 sts)

ROWS 20 AND 21: Rep Rows 2 and 3.

ROW 22 (RS, INCREASE/JOINING ROW): Replace MC st on hook, ch 3, *dc in next 3 sts, 2 dc in next st, dc in next 4 sts; rep from * to last 6 sts, dc in next 3 sts, 2 dc in next st, dc in last 2 sts, turn. (215 sts)

ROWS 23 AND 24: Rep Rows 2 and 3.

ROW 25 (INCREASE ROW, RS): Replace MC st on hook, ch 3, dc in same st, *dc in next 8 sts, 2 dc in next st; rep from * to last 7 sts, dc in last 7 sts, turn. (239 sts)

ROW 26: Rep Row 2.

ROW 27: With B, Rep Row 3.

ROW 28 (INCREASE ROW, RS): Replace MC st on hook, ch 3, *2 dc in next st, dc in next 9 sts; rep from * to last 8 sts, 2 dc in next st, dc in last 7 sts, turn. (263 sts)

ROWS 29 AND 30: Rep Rows 2 and 3.

ROW 31 (INCREASE ROW, RS): Replace MC st on hook, ch 3, dc in same st, *dc in next 10 sts, 2 dc in next st; rep from * to last 9 sts, dc in last 9 sts, turn. (287 sts)

ROWS 32 AND 33: Rep Rows 2 and 3.

ROW 34 (RS, INCREASE/JOINING ROW): Replace MC st on hook, ch 3, *2 dc in next st, dc in next 11 sts; rep from * to last 10 sts, 2 dc in next st, dc in last 9 sts, turn. (311 sts)

ROW 35: Rep Row 2.

ROW 36: With B, rep Row 3.

ROW 37 (RS, INCREASE/JOINING ROW): Replace MC st on hook, ch 3, dc in same st, *dc in next 12 sts, 2 dc in next st; rep from * to last 11 sts, dc in last 11 sts, turn. (335 sts)

ROWS 38 AND 39: Rep Rows 2 and 3.

ROW 40 (RS, INCREASE/JOINING ROW): Replace MC st on hook, ch 3, *2 dc in next st, dc in next 13 sts; rep from * to last 12 sts, 2 dc in next st, dc in last 11 sts, turn. (359 sts)

ROWS 41 AND 42: Rep Rows 2 and 3.

ROW 43 (RS, JOINING ROW): Replace MC st on hook, ch 3, dc in each st and ch-1 space across; *do not turn.*

EDGING

ROW 1: Ch 1, sc evenly down edge of piece to foundation ch, 2 sc in corner st, sc in free loop of each foundation ch across, 2 sc in corner st, sc evenly down edge to beginning of last row; *do not turn.* Fasten off.

ROW 2 (RS): With C, standing sc in first st of Row 43, ch 1, skip 1 sc, sc in next sc; rep from * across to corner; *do not turn.* Fasten off.

ROW 3 (RS): With B, (standing sc, ch 3, 2 dc) in first space of previous row; *(sc, ch 3, 2 dc) in next space; rep from * across, slip st in last space. Fasten off.

FINISHING

► Weave in ends.

For the
Home

Beautiful Bows

DESIGNED BY BARBARA KREUTER

CHRISTMAS IS A SEASON FOR RIBBONS tied in bows! We use them on pretty packages to give to our loved ones. We decorate garlands, wreaths, and trees with more bows. Tunisian Cross Stitch creates textures that look woven — ideal for creating ribbonlike pieces, in exactly the shades and sizes we want. A lightweight wire helps the ribbon keep its shape. Three very different types of yarn demonstrate the versatility of this single pattern.

FINISHED MEASUREMENTS

- ▶ Small: 5"/12.5 cm wide, 4"/10 cm high, tied
- ▶ Medium: 7"/18 cm wide, 6½"/16.5 high, tied
- ▶ Large: 9½"/24 cm wide, 12"/30.5 cm high, tied

YARN

- ▶ Small: Nazli Gelin Garden 10, (0), size 10 crochet thread, 100% cotton, 308 yds/281.5 m, 1.75 oz/50 g, 1 ball Color 700-14
- ▶ Medium: Claudia Hand Painted Yarns Addiction, (1), 100% wool, 175 yds/160 m, 1.75 oz/50 g, 1 skein Color Peony
- ▶ Large: Berroco Lustra, (4), 50% wool/50% tencel, 197 yds/180 m, 3.5 oz/100 g, 1 skein Color 3184 Bordeaux

CROCHET HOOK

For the small and medium bows, a regular straight crochet hook without a thumb grip may be substituted for a Tunisian hook.

▶ Small: US E/4 (3.5 mm) hook, US B/1 (2.25 mm) Tunisian hook

▶ Medium: US I/9 (5.5 mm) hook, US G/6 (4 mm) Tunisian hook

▶ Large: US L/11 (8 mm) hook, US J/10 (6 mm) Tunisian hook *or size needed to obtain correct gauge*

GAUGE

With smaller (Tunisian) hook

▶ Small: 36 sts and 34 rows = 4"/10 cm in TSS

▶ Medium: 25 sts and 20 rows = 4"/10 cm in TSS

▶ Large: 16 sts and 13 rows = 4"/10 cm in TSS

OTHER SUPPLIES

▶ Yarn needle

▶ 28-gauge wire

▶ Beading pliers or other wire-cutting tool to trim and bend wire

▶ ½"/1.25 cm plastic rings (optional)

▶ Sewing needle and thread (optional)

● PROJECT NOTES ●

▶ The bow is worked in Tunisian Simple Stitch, using short rows to create notched ends. Instructions are written for right-handed crocheters with changes for left-handed crocheters in brackets [ ].

▶ The two edges of the ribbon-like piece may not remain the same length, which can cause arcing of the piece. To keep the right edge from growing too much, pull gently on working yarn when there are 2 loops on hook to take out any slack. To keep the left edge from pulling in too much, work the last stitch of the forward pass and the first stitch of the return pass more loosely than regular tension.

▶ Instructions are the same for all bow sizes. The differences in size are a result of using different weights of yarn.

PATTERN ESSENTIALS

ES (Edge Stitch)
At left [right] edge on forward pass, pull up 1 loop under the final post together with the post immediately behind it.

TCS (Tunisian Cross Stitch)
Skip next vertical bar, insert hook under next vertical bar, yarnover, pull up loop, insert hook from right to left [left to right] under last skipped vertical bar. (2 loops added) Work standard return pass unless otherwise noted.

TSS2tog (Tunisian Simple Stitch 2 together)
Insert hook under next 2 vertical bars, yarnover, pull up loop. (1 loop added) Work standard return pass unless otherwise noted.

TUNISIAN SIMPLE STITCH (TSS)

See page 176 for illustrations of how to work this stitch.

Chain desired number.

ROW 1: Insert hook in 2nd ch from hook, yarnover and pull up a loop, (insert hook into next ch, yarnover, pull up a loop) across: *forward pass complete;* yarnover, pull through 1 loop on hook, (yarnover, pull through 2 loops on hook) across (1 loop remains and counts as first st of next row): *standard return pass complete.*

ROW 2: Skip first vertical bar, insert hook under next vertical bar, yarnover, pull up loop, (insert hook under next vertical bar, yarnover, pull up loop) across (1 loop remains and counts as first st of next row); work loops off using standard return pass as for Row 1.

Rep Row 2 for pattern.

Bow

FIRST NOTCHED END

Chart Key

FORWARD SYMBOLS

0   loop on hook at beg of row; also ch 1 at beg of Top Edging

| TSS (or ES at end of row)

✕   TCS

∧   TSS2tog

RETURN SYMBOLS

~   loop on hook at beg of row; also ch 1 at beg of Top Edging

Bottom Edging

FIRST NOTCHED END

Note: Work standard return pass unless otherwise noted.

▶ With larger regular hook, ch 17. Change to smaller (Tunisian) hook (used for gauge).

SHORT ROW 1: Sc in 2nd ch from hook. (1 sc)

SHORT ROW 2: Insert hook from front to back under left-most [right-most] strand of sc, yarnover, pull up loop, pull up 1 loop in next ch (3 loops); work return pass. (You now have three vertical bars: 1 from the turning ch, 1 from the sc, and 1 from the TSS.)

SHORT ROW 3: TCS 1, pull up 1 loop in next ch (4 loops); work return pass.

SHORT ROW 4: TCS 1, TSS 1, pull up 1 loop in next ch (5 loops); work return pass.

SHORT ROW 5: TCS 1, TSS 2, pull up 1 loop in next ch (6 loops); work return pass.

SHORT ROW 6: TCS 1, TSS 3, pull up 1 loop in next ch (7 loops); work return pass.

SHORT ROW 7: TCS 1, TSS 4, pull up 1 loop in next ch (8 loops); work return pass.

SHORT ROW 8: TCS 1, TSS 5, pull up 1 loop in each of remaining 9 chs (17 loops); yarnover and pull through 1 loop, yarnover and pull through 2 loops, do not work off remaining sts. (16 loops remain on hook)

SHORT ROW 9: ES (17 loops); yarnover and pull through 1 loop, (yarnover and pull through 2 loops) twice, do not work off remaining sts. (15 loops remain on hook)

SHORT ROW 10: TSS 1, ES (17 loops); yarnover and pull through 1 loop, (yarnover and pull through 2 loops) three times, do not work off remaining sts. (14 loops remain on hook)

SHORT ROW 11: TCS 1, ES (17 loops); yarnover and pull through 1 loop, (yarnover and pull through 2 loops) four times, do not work off remaining sts. (13 loops on hook remain on hook)

SHORT ROW 12: TSS 1, TCS 1, ES (17 loops); yo and pull through 1 loop, (yarnover and pull through 2 loops) five times, do not work off remaining sts. (12 loops remain on hook)

SHORT ROW 13: TSS 2, TCS 1, ES (17 loops); yarnover and pull through 1 loop, (yarnover and pull through 2 loops) six times, do not work off remaining sts. (11 loops remain on hook)

SHORT ROW 14: TSS 3, TCS 1, ES (17 loops); work return pass. (1 loop on hook)

ROW 15: TCS 1, TSS 5, TSS2tog, TSS 4, TCS 1, ES (16 loops); work return pass.

RIBBON

ROW 16: TCS 1, TSS 10, TCS 1, ES (16 loops); work return pass.

▶ Rep Row 16 until piece measures 21 (31, 46)"/53, (79, 117) cm or desired length.

SECOND NOTCHED END

SHORT ROW 1: TCS 1, TSS 5 (8 loops); *return pass:* *yarnover and pull through 2 loops; rep from * to end.

SHORT ROW 2: TCS 1, TSS 3, TSS2tog (7 loops); *yarnover and pull through 2 loops; rep from * to end.

Chart Key

FORWARD SYMBOLS

0   loop on hook at beg of row; also ch 1 at beg of Top Edging

| TSS (or ES at end of row)

✕   TCS

∧   TSS2tog

RETURN SYMBOLS

~   yo, draw through 1 lp for first st, yo, draw though 2 lps for each rem st

~   yo, draw through 2 lps at beg of return pass

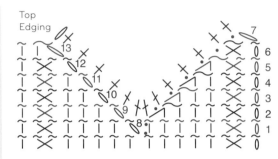

Top Edging

SHORT ROW 3: TCS 1, TSS 2, TSS2tog (6 loops); *yo and pull through 2 loops; rep from * to end.

SHORT ROW 4: TCS 1, TSS 1, TSS2tog (5 loops); *yo and pull through 2 loops; rep from * to end.

SHORT ROW 5: TCS 1, TSS2tog (4 loops); *yo and pull through 2 loops; rep from * to end.

SHORT ROW 6: TCS 1 (3 loops); *yo and pull through 2 loops; rep from * to end.

SHORT ROW 7: Ch 1, slip st in each st of diagonal ending with slip st in last post used on Short Row 1, TSS 5, TCS 1, ES (9 loops remain on hook); work return pass.

SHORT ROW 8: Skip next vertical bar, TSS 4, TCS 1, ES (8 loops remain on hook); work return pass.

SHORT ROW 9: Skip next vertical bar, TSS 3, TCS 1, ES (7 loops remain on hook); work return pass.

SHORT ROW 10: Skip next vertical bar, TSS 2, TCS 1, ES (6 loops remain on hook); work return pass.

SHORT ROW 11: Skip next vertical bar, TSS 1, TCS 1, ES (5 loops remain on hook); work return pass.

SHORT ROW 12: Skip next vertical bar, TCS 1, ES (4 loops remain on hook); work return pass.

SHORT ROW 13: Skip next vertical bar, TSS 1, ES (3 loops remain on hook); yo and pull through 1 loop, yo and pull through 3 loops. Turn, ch 1, sc in each st of notched edge for top edging.

▸ Fasten off.

BOTTOM EDGING

▸ With wrong side facing, working across opposite side of foundation ch, join yarn with standing sc in first ch, work 1 sc in each ch across first notched edge. Fasten off.

FINISHING

▸ Weave in ends. Steam block lightly.

▸ Cut 2 pieces of wire each 2"/5 cm longer than edge of piece. With wrong side facing, run a wire through backs of TCS sts along one edge, checking that wire does not show on right side of work; do not finish ends of wire until after tying bow. Wire other edge the same way.

▸ Tie bow. Using wire-cutting pliers, finish each wire end by clipping to ⅜"/1 cm and bending in half against main length of wire to make the finished end smooth, not scratchy.

▸ If desired for attaching bow to ornament hanger, garland, or package, sew 1 or 2 plastic rings to back of knot using sewing thread.

Tabletop Trees

HERE'S A WINTRY TRIO that will outlast the Christmas season. It will look fantastic on a mantel, as a table center-piece, or on a desk. The snowy embellishment will cover any imperfect stitching, making it a good project for the beginning-to-intermediate crocheter. Even variations in the snowy stuff will only make it look more authentic.

FINISHED MEASUREMENTS

▸ 7 (8, 9)"/18, (20.5, 23) cm tall

YARN

▸ Plymouth Yarn Cleo (3), 100% mercerized pima cotton, 125 yds/114 m, 1.75 oz/50 g, 2 skeins Color 181 Silver (A)

▸ Grignasco Knits Kid Seta (2), 70% super kid mohair, 30% silk, 230 yds/210 m, .88 oz/25 g, 2 balls Color 416 white (B)

CROCHET HOOKS

▸ US F/5 (3.75 mm) for tree inner layer *or size needed to obtain correct gauge*

▸ US E/4 (3.5 mm) for tree outer layer

GAUGE

▸ With larger hook and A, 20 sts and 10 rnds = 4"/10 cm in back loop double crochet

OTHER SUPPLIES

▸ Stitch marker

▸ Yarn needle

▸ 650 Size 8 silver-colored glass seed beads

▸ Bead needle, sewing thread, bead threader

▸ File folders or light card stock for lining

▸ Cellophane tape (optional)

PATTERN ESSENTIALS

b-ch (bead chain)
Yarnover, push bead up to hook, pull yarn through.

bead picot-3
Ch 1, yarnover, push bead up to hook, pull yarn through, ch 1, slip st in 3rd ch from hook.

BLdc (back loop double crochet)
Work 1 double crochet into the back loop only.

BLhdc (back loop half double crochet)
Work 1 half double crochet into the back loop only.

BLsc (back loop single crochet)
Work 1 single crochet into the back loop only.

Picot-3
Ch1, slip st in 3rd ch from hook.

> ● **PROJECT NOTE** ●
>
> ▶ The trees are worked top-down in the round without joining rounds, working in the back loops only. After the inner layer is complete, the snowy outer layer stitches are worked into the front loops of each stitch, working from base to top, with beads added as desired.

Large Tree

INNER LAYER

▸ With A, ch 4, join with slip st to form a ring.

RND 1: Ch 3 (counts as dc), 7 dc in ring; do not join. (8 dc) Place marker in the first st of the rnd and move it up as you work each rnd. *Work in back loops of each st around from this point to the last round.*

RND 2: *2 BLdc in next dc, BLdc in next dc; rep from * around. (12 BLdc)

RND 3: Rep Rnd 2. (18 BLdc)

INNER LAYER, RNDS 1-3

RND 4 AND ALL EVEN-NUMBERED RNDS: BLdc in each dc around.

RND 5: *2 BLdc in next dc, BLdc in next 2 dc; rep from * around. (24 BLdc)

RND 7: *BLdc in next 2 dc, 2 BLdc in next dc, BLdc in next dc; rep from * around. (30 BLdc)

RND 9: *BLdc in next st, 2 BLdc in next dc, BLdc in next 3 dc; rep from * around. (36 BLdc)

RND 11: *2 BLdc in next dc, BLdc in next 5 dc; rep from * around. (42 BLdc)

RND 13: *BLdc in next 2 dc, 2 BLdc in next dc, BLdc in next 4 dc; rep from * around. (48 BLdc)

RND 15: *BLdc in next dc, 2 BLdc in next dc, BLdc in next 6 dc; rep from * around. (54 BLdc)

RND 17: *2 BLdc in next dc, BLdc in next 8 dc; rep from * around. (60 BLdc)

RND 19: *BLdc in next 5 dc, 2 BLdc in next dc, BLdc in next 4 dc; rep from * around. (66 BLdc)

RND 21: Place marker in next st and leave in place until outer layer is complete. BLdc in next 44 sts, BLhdc in next 4 sts, BLsc in each st to end.

RND 22: Sc in both loops of each st around, slip st in both loops of
next 3 sts.

▸ Fasten off. Weave in ends.

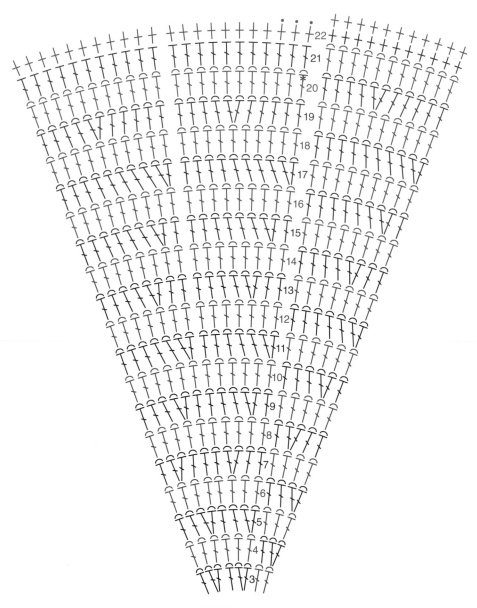

LARGE TREE
INNER LAYERS, RNDS 3-22

OUTER LAYER

▸ Work in free loops of Inner Layer dc sts throughout. Join B with slip st two sts before marked st near bottom of tree, sc in next st, *picot-3, dc in next st; rep from * around, ending with dc in last free loop at top of tree; *do not fasten off.*

▸ String 11 beads onto B. Beginning with a slip knot on hook, ch 1, (bead picot-3) 11 times. Fasten off leaving a 6"/15 cm tail. (*top embellishment made*)

▸ Use yarn tail to gather top embellishment into a spiral to cover remaining Outer Layer sts at top of tree. Sew in place. Weave in ends.

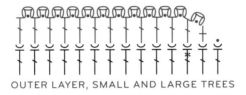

OUTER LAYER, SMALL AND LARGE TREES

GARLAND

▸ String 530 beads onto B. (See page 177.)

▸ With B and smaller hook, *ch 3, b-ch, rep from * until all beads are used up. Fasten off.

▸ Using photo as a guide, drape garland loosely around tree. Weave beginning and ending tails on wrong side of Outer Layer. With 3"/7.5 cm lengths of B, tie garland onto picots using a square knot. Trim ends close to knot, working carefully to avoid cutting crochet stitches.

MAKING THE LINING

▶ Roll a file folder or piece of light card stock into a cone shape (A). Insert cone into tree (B), and draw a line on the folder around the bottom of the tree. Remove folder. Cut along the curved line on the file folder (C). Reroll folder, and tape into shape, if desired (D). Insert cone into tree.

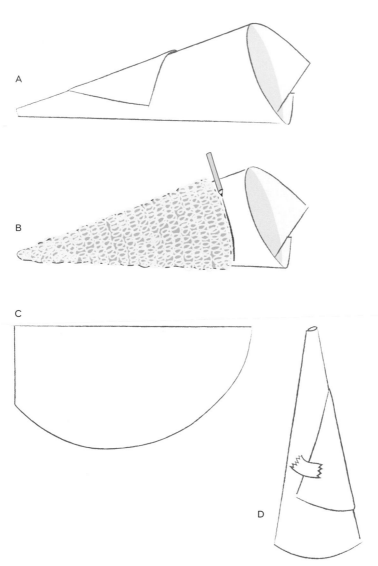

A

B

C

D

Medium Tree

INNER LAYER

▸ Make as for Large Tree Inner Layer through Rnd 16.

RND 17: Place marker in next st and leave in place until branches are complete. BLdc in next 36 sts, BLhdc in next 4 sts, BLsc in each st to end.

RND 18: Sc in both loops of each st around, slip st in both loops of next 3 sts.

▸ Fasten off. Weave in ends.

OUTER LAYER

▸ Note: The following instructions place beads in every 5th picot to create a semi-random look; adjust this rate if beads begin stacking in a vertical line. See symbol chart below.

▸ String 100 beads onto B. Work in free loops of Inner Layer dc sts throughout.

▸ Join B with slip st two sts before marked st near bottom of tree, sc in next st, dc in next st, *bead picot-3, dc in next st, (picot-3, dc in next st) four times; rep from * to l st from end, sc in last free loop at top of tree; *do not fasten off.* Bead picot-3, (picot-3) four times, ch 1. (*top embellishment made*)

▸ Fasten off, leaving a 6"/15 cm tail. Remove marker.

▸ Use yarn tail to gather top embellishment into a spiral to cover remaining Inner Layer sts at top of tree. Sew in place. Weave in ends.

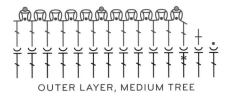

OUTER LAYER, MEDIUM TREE

LINING

▸ Make as for Large Tree.

Small Tree

INNER LAYER

▸ Make as for Large Tree through Rnd 14.

RND 15: Place marker in next st and leave in place until Outer Layer is complete. BLdc in next 32 sts, BLhdc in next 4 sts, BLsc in each st to end.

RND 16: Sc in both loops of each st around, slip st in both loops of next 3 sts.

▸ Fasten off. Weave in ends.

OUTER LAYER

▸ Work in free loops of Inner Layer dc sts throughout. Join B with slip st two sts before marked st near bottom of tree, sc in next st, *picot-3, dc in next st; rep from * around, ending with dc in last free loop at top of tree; *do not fasten off.** (Picot-3) nine times, ch 1. (*top embellishment made*). See page 131 for stitch chart.

▸ Fasten off, leaving a 6"/15 cm tail. Remove marker.

▸ Use yarn tail to gather top embellishment into a spiral to cover remaining Inner Layer sts at top of tree. Sew in place. Weave in ends.

LINING

▸ Make as for Large Tree.

Advent Garland

WHAT COULD BE COZIER THAN SOCKS AND MITTENS hung up to dry by the fireplace? Pint-sized versions of these woolly favorites hold tiny treats to help count down the days until Christmas. Use your most colorful leftover yarns and the patterns given here to make your own one-of-a-kind Advent garland.

FINISHED MEASUREMENTS

- Each sock is about 2"/5 cm wide and 4½–5"/11.5–12.5 cm long
- Each mitten is about 2¼"/6 cm wide and 3½–4½"/9–11.5 cm long
- Sizes of socks and mittens may vary.

YARN

- Brown Sheep NatureSpun Sport, (2), 100% wool, 184 yds/168 m, 3.5 oz/100 g, 1 skein each Color 116S Blue Boy (A), 305S Impasse Yellow (B), 730S Natural (C), 112S Elf Green (D), N46S Red Fox (E), 108S Cherry Delight (F), N78S Turquoise Wonder (G)

CROCHET HOOKS

- US E/4 (3.5 mm) and F/5 (3.75 mm)
- Steel size 12 (1 mm) for placing beads

GAUGE

- 5 sts and 6 rnds = 1"/2.5 cm in single crochet with E/4 (3.5 mm) hook
- 4 sts and 5 rnds = 1"/2.5 cm in single crochet with F/5 (3.75 mm) hook
- Gauge is not critical for this project (but see note, page 9). Use smaller or larger hook to vary the size of the pieces.

OTHER SUPPLIES

- Yarn needle
- 60 Size 6 glass seed beads in green
- One 1¼"/3 cm heart button (JHB International #21591)
- Bead needle and bead threader
- Sewing needle and thread to match E
- Three ¾"/2 cm pink buttons
- 60 Size 6 glass Delica beads in green

PATTERN ESSENTIALS

BPdc (back post double crochet)
Yarnover, insert hook from back to front to back around post of next stitch and pull up a loop, (yarnover and pull through two loops on hook) two times.

BPhdc (back post half double crochet)
Yarnover, insert hook from back to front to back around post of next stitch and pull up a loop, yarnover and pull through three loops on hook.

FPdc (front post double crochet)
Yarnover, insert hook from front to back to front around post of stitch indicated and pull up a loop, (yarnover and pull through two loops on hook) two times.

FPhdc (front post half double crochet)
Yarnover, insert hook from front to back to front around post of stitch indicated and pull up a loop, yarnover and pull through three loops on hook.

pb (place bead)
Drop loop from hook, insert steel hook through bead and into dropped loop, pull loop through bead and snug bead up to last stitch completed, replace loop onto hook.

sc2tog (single crochet 2 stitches together)
(Insert hook into next st and pull up a loop) two times, yarnover and pull through all 3 loops on hook.

standing sc (standing single crochet)
Beginning with slip knot on hook, insert hook into stitch or space indicated, yarnover, pull up a loop, yarnover and pull through both loops on hook.

tight picot-2
Ch 2, slip st in stitch at base of chain.

• PROJECT NOTES •

► The socks are worked in rounds from the toe up. The heel is worked after the foot and leg are complete.

► Change color for the next round on the last stitch of the round, as follows: With old color, insert hook into stitch and pull up a loop; with new color, yarnover and pull through both loops on hook to complete the stitch.

► The end-of-round joins may be worked in the familiar way (slip stitch in first st of round) or as follows: Drop loop from hook, insert hook from front to back into first st of round, pick up dropped loop and pull it through.

► The mitten thumb and hand are worked from the top down in rounds without joining. The thumb is worked first. After the hand is complete, the thumb is joined and the mitten is worked down to the cuff.

Socks

No.1

No.2

No.3

No.4

No.5

No.6

No.7

No.8

No.9

No.10

No.11

No.12

Sock №1

TOE

▸ With G, chain 2.

RND 1: 6 sc in 2nd ch from hook, join to first sc. (6 sc)

RND 2: Ch 1, 2 sc in each sc around, join to first sc. (12 sc)

RND 3: Ch 1, *sc in next sc, 2 sc in next sc; rep from * around, join to first sc. (18 sc)

RND 4: Ch 1, sc in each sc around; join to first sc.

RND 5: Ch 1, sc in each sc around; with F, join to first sc. Cut G.

FOOT

RNDS 1–6: With F, ch 1, sc in each sc around, join to first sc. Fasten off.

LEG

RND 1: With F, ch 4, skip first 4 sc Rnd 6 of Foot, sc in next 9 sc, ch 5, skip next 5 sc, join with slip st to first ch.

RND 2: Ch 1, sc in each sc and in each ch around, join to first sc. (18 sc)

RNDS 3–11: Work 9 more rnds even in sc, changing to G at end of Rnd 11.

RND 12: With G, ch 1, sc in each sc around, join to first sc, ch 8, slip st in same st for hanging loop.

▸ Fasten off.

HEEL

RND 1: With G and RS facing, standing sc in heel opening at center back leg, sc in each st around and sc in side of each sc at corners of heel, join with slip st to first sc. (20 sc)

RND 2: Ch 1, sc in next 2 sc, sc2tog; rep from * around, join to first sc. (15 sc)

RND 3: Ch 1, sc2tog, sc in next sc; rep from * around, join with slip st to first sc. (10 sc)

HEEL, *continued*

RND 4: Ch 1, sc2tog around, join with slip st to first sc. (5 sc)

▸ Fasten off. Thread tail through sts and pull tight to close hole.

FINISHING

▸ Using yarn tails, close gaps at heel corners. Weave in ends.

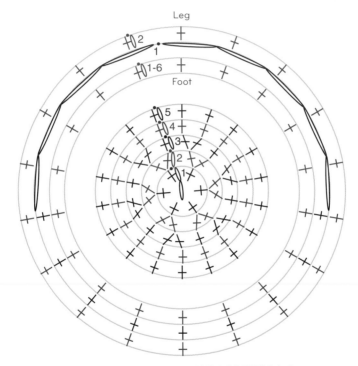

SOCK No.1 TOE, FOOT AND LEG RNDS 1–2

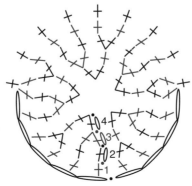

SOCK No.1 HEEL

Sock №2

▸ Work as for Sock #1, working Toe, Foot, and Leg in D and Final Rnd and Heel in B.

Sock №3

▸ Work as for Sock #1, working Toe, Foot, and Leg in F and Final Rnd and Heel in B.

▸ Cut three 4"/10 cm lengths of each of B, C, F and G. Holding 1 strand of each color together, attach three groups of fringe along top of sock, using photo as a guide. Trim ends.

Sock №4

▸ Work as for Sock #1, working Toe, Foot, and Leg in G and Final Rnd and Heel in B.

▸ With F and using photo as a guide, surface chain (see page 176) between second and third rounds at top of stocking, and a similar distance around heel.

Sock №5

▸ Work as for Sock #1, working Toe, Foot, and Leg in C and Final Rnd and Heel in B.

Sock №6

▸ Work as for Sock #1, working Toe, Heel, and Final Rnd in C and Foot and Leg in E. With sewing needle and thread, using photo as a guide, sew 18 seed beads evenly spaced around Rnd 1 of Foot, 18 seed beads evenly spaced around Rnd 11 of Leg, and 18–20 seed beads evenly spaced around Heel.

Sock №7

TOE AND FOOT

▸ With A, work same as Sock #1, working 3 rnds with A, 1 rnd each of C, F, C; 2 rnds A; 1 rnd each of C, F, and C. Fasten off.

LEG

RND 1: With A, ch 4, skip first 4 sc of Rnd 11 of Foot, sc in next 9 sc, ch 5, skip next 5 sc, join to first ch.

RND 2: Ch 1, sc in each sc and in each ch around; with C, join to first sc. (18 sc)

RNDS 3–10: Rep Rnds 4–11 of Foot, changing to A on last rnd.

RND 11: With A, sc in each sc around.

RND 12: With A, ch 1, sc in each sc around, join with slip st to first sc, ch 8, slip st in same st.

▸ Fasten off.

HEEL

▸ With A, work as for Sock #1.

FINISHING

▸ Using yarn tails, close gaps at heel corners. Weave in ends.

Sock №8

▸ Work as for Sock #1, working Heel, Final Rnd, and first three rounds of Toe in F. Work remainder of Toe and Foot in 1-rnd stripes of G, C, F, and B. Work Rnd 1 of Leg in G (next color in stripe sequence), then continue in established stripe pattern for remainder of Leg.

Sock №9

TOE

▸ With A, work Rnds 1–4 as for Sock #1.

RND 5: Ch 1, sc in each sc around; with E, join with slip st to back loop of first sc. Cut A.

FOOT

RND 1: With E, ch 1, sc in each sc around; with B, join with slip st to back loop of first sc.

RND 2: With B, ch 1, BLsc in each sc around; with G, join with slip st to back loop of first sc.

RNDS 3–5: Rep Rnd 2, working in the following color sequence: 1 rnd each of G, C and F.

▶ Fasten off.

LEG

RND 1: With A, ch 4, skip first 4 sts of Foot, BLsc in next 9 sc, ch 5, skip next 5 sts; with E, join with slip st to first ch.

RND 2: With E, ch 1, BLsc in each BLsc and sc in back bump of each ch around; with B, join with slip st to first sc. (18 sc)

RNDS 3–12: Work even in sc, working in the following color sequence: 1 rnd each of *B, G, C, F*, A, E, rep from * to * once.

FINAL RND: With A, ch 1, BLsc in each st around, join with slip st to first sc, ch 8, slip st in same st for hanging loop.

▶ Fasten off.

HEEL

▶ With A, work as for Sock #1.

FINISHING

▶ Using yarn tails, close gaps at heel corners. Weave in ends.

Sock №10

▶ Work as for Sock #1, working Toe, Heel, and Final Round in E and Foot and Leg in D. With D, sew heart button on leg.

Sock №11

TOE

▶ With E, work as for Sock #1 through Rnd 5. Do not cut E.

FOOT

RND 1: With D, ch 1, sc in same st, *ch 1, skip 1 sc, sc in next sc; rep from * to last st, ch 1, skip 1 sc, join with slip st to first sc. Drop D from hook.

RND 2: Draw up a loop of E in first space of previous rnd, ch 1, sc in same space, *ch 1, sc in next space; rep from * to last st, join with sc to first sc.

RND 3: Ch 1, sc in space formed by joining sc, *ch 1, sc in next space; rep from * to last st, ch 1, skip 1 sc, join with slip st to first sc. Drop E from hook.

RND 4: Draw up a loop of D in last space of previous round, ch 1, sc in same space, *ch 1, sc in next space; rep from * to last st, ch 1, skip 1 sc, join with slip st to first sc. Fasten off D.

RNDS 5 AND 6: Rep Rnds 2 and 3.

▶ Fasten off E.

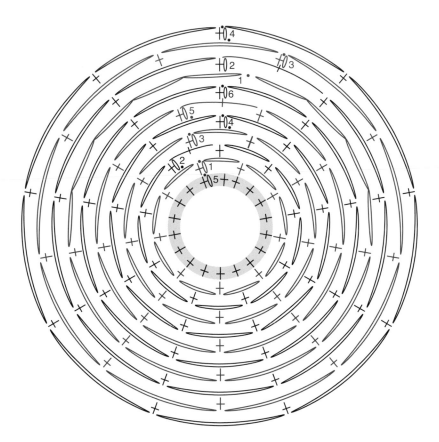

SOCK No.11 TOE, FOOT AND LEG RNDS 1–4

LEG

RND 1: With E, ch 5, skip 5 sts (counting ch-1 space as a st), (sc in next space, ch 1) four times, sc in next space, ch 4, skip 4 sts, join with slip st to first ch.

RND 2: Ch 1, sc in first ch, (ch 1, skip 1 ch, sc in next ch) two times, (ch 1, sc in next space) four times, ch 1, sc in next ch, ch 1, skip 1 ch, sc in next ch, skip 1 ch, join with sc to first sc.

RND 3: Ch 1, sc in space formed by joining sc, ch 1, *sc in next space, ch 1; rep from * around, join with slip st to first sc. Drop E from hook.

RND 4: Draw up a loop of D in first space of previous round, ch 1, sc in same space, *ch 1, sc in next space; rep from * to last st, ch 1, skip 1 sc, join with slip st to first sc. Drop D from hook.

RND 5: Draw up a loop of E in last space of previous rnd, ch 1, sc in same space, *ch 1, sc in next space; rep from * around, join with sc to first sc.

RND 6: Ch 1, sc in space formed by joining sc, *ch 1, sc in next space; rep from * to last st, ch 1, skip 1 sc, join with slip st to first sc. Drop E from hook.

RND 7: Draw up a loop of D in first space of previous round, ch 1, sc in same space, *ch 1, sc in next space; rep from * to last st, ch 1, skip 1 sc, join with slip st to first sc.

RNDS 8–10: Rep Rnds 5–7. Fasten off D.

RNDS 11 AND 12: Rep Rnds 5 and 6, but do not drop E from hook.

FINAL RND: Ch 1, sc in each sc and ch-1 space around, join with slip st to first sc, ch 8, slip st in same st.

▶ Fasten off.

HEEL

▶ With D, work as for Sock #1. Weave in ends.

Sock №12

▶ Work as for Sock #11, using A as main color and B as contrasting color. Work Heel with B.

Mittens

No.1

No.2

No.3

No.4

No.5

No.6

No.7

No.8

No.9

No.10

No.11

No.12

Mitten №1

THUMB

▸ With G, begin with an adjustable ring (see page 171).

RND 1: Ch 1, 4 sc in ring; *do not join.* (4 sc) Place marker in first st of round and move up each round.

RND 2: (Sc in next sc, 2 sc in next sc) two times. (6 sc)

RNDS 3 AND 4: Sc in each sc around.

▸ Fasten off.

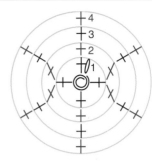

HAND

▸ With G, begin with an adjustable ring.

RND 1: Ch 1, 6 sc in ring; *do not join.* (6 sc) Place marker in first st of round and move it up each round.

RND 2: 2 sc in each sc around. (12 sc)

RND 3: *Sc in next sc, 2 sc in next sc; rep from * around. (18 sc)

RNDS 4–11: Sc in each sc around.

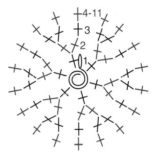

GUSSET

RND 1 (JOIN THUMB): Sc in each sc around, sc in each sc around thumb. (24 sc) Place marker in first st of round and move it up each round.

RNDS 2 AND 3: Sc in each sc to last 4 sc, sc2tog, sc in last 2 sc. (22 sc at end of last rnd)

RNDS 4 AND 5: Sc in each sc to last 3 sc, sc2tog, sc in last sc. (20 sc)

RNDS 6 AND 7: Sc in each sc to last 2 sts, sc2tog. (18 sc at end of last rnd)

▸ **RND 8:** Sc in each sc around.

RND 1: Ch 2 (does not count as a st), (FPdc, BPdc) eight times, FPhdc, BPhdc, join with slip st to first FPdc. Fasten off.

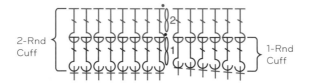

2-Rnd Cuff   1-Rnd Cuff

FINISHING

▸ Using yarn tails, close gaps at base of thumb. Weave in ends.

▸ Using photo as a guide, use a short length of B to tie three ¾"/2 cm pink buttons in a straight line on back of hand. Trim ends of B.

Mitten №2

▸ With B, work as for Mitten #1, but do not fasten off last rnd of Cuff. Continue as follows after Rnd 1 of Cuff:

RND 2: Ch 2, *FPdc in next FPdc, BPdc in next BPdc; rep from * around, join with slip st to first FPdc. Fasten off.

Mitten №3

▸ With C, work Thumb, Hand, and Gusset as for Mitten #1; work Cuff in E.

Mitten №4

▸ With A, work Thumb, Hand, and Gusset as for Mitten #1; work Cuff in B.

STAR

▸ Leaving a 6"/15 cm tail of B, begin with an adjustable ring. (Ch 2, dc, tight picot-2, ch 2, slip st) five times in ring. Fasten off. Pull beginning tail to close center. Fasten off.

FINISHING

▸ Using yarn tails, close gaps at base of thumb and sew star to back of hand. Weave in ends.

Mitten №5

▸ Work as for Mitten #2, making Thumb and Cuff (2 rnds) in E, and working Hand and Gusset in alternating 1-rnd strips of E and C.

Mitten №6

▸ With F, work Thumb and Hand as for Rnds 1–4 of Mitten #1.

RND 5: With C, *sc in next st, dc in rnd below next st, skip st behind dc just made; rep from * around.

RNDS 6 AND 7: With F, sc in each sc around.

RNDS 8–10: Rep Rnds 5–7.

RND 11: Rep Rnd 5. Cut C.

▸ With F, work Gusset and Cuff as for Mitten #1.

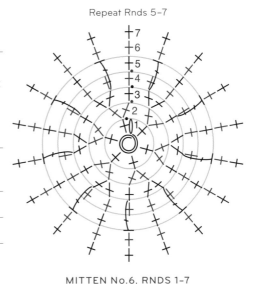

Repeat Rnds 5–7

MITTEN No.6, RNDS 1–7

Mitten №7

▸ With B, work as for Mitten #1. With F and G, work freeform surface crochet lines over entire mitten, using photo as a guide.

Mitten №8

▸ Work as for Mitten #2, making Thumb and Cuff (2 rnds) in A, and Hand and Gusset in 1-rnd strips of A, C, D, E and B.

Mitten №9

▸ Work as for Mitten #1, making Thumb in F, Cuff in G, and Hand and Gusset in 2-rnd stripes of G, B and F.

Mitten №10

▸ With D, work Thumb and Hand Rnds 1–4 of Mitten #1.

RND 5: With C, *sc in next st, dc in row below next st, skip st behind dc just made; rep from * around.

RNDS 6 AND 7: With D, sc in each sc around.

RND 8: With E, rep Rnd 5. Cut E.

RNDS 9–10: Rep Rnds 6–7.

RND 11: With C, rep Rnd 5. Cut C.

▸ With D, work Gusset and Cuff as for Mitten #1.

Mitten №11

▸ With E, work as for Mitten #1. With yarn needle and A and B, stitch running threads vertically down mitten, using photo as a guide.

Mitten №12

▸ String 60 Delica beads onto F. (See page 177.) With F, work Thumb and Rnds 1–3 of Hand as for Mitten #1.

RND 4: *Sc in next sc, pb, sc in next 2 sc; rep from * around.

RNDS 5, 7 AND 9: Sc in each sc around.

RND 6: *Sc in next 3 sc, pb; rep from * around.

RND 8: *Sc in next 2 sc, pb, sc in next sc; rep from * around.

RND 10: Rep Rnd 5.

▸ Fasten off.

GUSSET

RND 1 (JOIN THUMB): Sc in each sc around, sc in each sc around thumb. (24 sc) Place marker in first st of round and move it up each round.

RND 2: (Sc in next 3 sc, pb) six times, sc in next 2 sc, sc2tog, sc in next 2 sc. (23 sc)

RND 3: Sc in each sc to last 4 sc, sc2tog, sc in last 2 sc. (22 sc)

RND 4: (Sc in next 2 sc, pb, sc in next sc) six times, sc2tog, sc in last sc. (21 sc)

RND 5: Sc in each sc to last 2 sc, sc2tog. (20 sc)

RND 6: (Sc in next sc, pb, sc in next 2 sc) six times, sc2tog. (19 sts)

RND 7: Rep Rnd 5. (18 sts)

RND 8: Sc in each sc around.

CUFF

RND 1: *Sc in next sc, pb; rep from * around.

RND 2: Sc in each sc around, slip st in first st.

▸ Fasten off.

FINISHING

▸ Cut two 5 yd./4.5 m strands each of C and E. Holding strands together, make twisted cord (see page 178). Attach socks and mittens to cord with ornament hangers, yarn, or tiny clothespins.

Snowflake Pillows

NINE SNOWFLAKES! As in nature, no two of these thread crochet snowflakes are alike. A large-scale snowflake is the focus of the round pillow, while delicate flakes float on an ice-blue sky in the square pillow. If you prefer, just sew snowflakes onto purchased pillows. Make extra snowflakes to hang on your tree or to decorate your gifts.

FINISHED MEASUREMENTS

- ▸ Round pillow: 16"/40.5 cm circumference
- ▸ Square pillow: 16"/40.5 cm square
- ▸ Giant Snowflake: 13½"/34.5 cm in diameter
- ▸ Snowflake Motifs #1 through 8: Range in size from 1⅛"/3 cm to 4"/10 cm

YARN

- ▸ Size 10 crochet thread, [●●], 100% cotton, 225 yds/206 m, 1 ball White

CROCHET HOOKS

- ▸ Steel 1.25 mm *or size needed to obtain correct gauge*

GAUGE

- ▸ First 3 rnds of giant Snowflake Motif measure 2½"/6.5 cm in diameter
- ▸ Snowflake Motif #1 measures 3¼"/8.5 cm in diameter after blocking
- ▸ Gauge for snowflake motifs varies and is not critical.

OTHER SUPPLIES

- ▸ Yarn needle
- ▸ 1 yard (1 m) fabric for pillow covers
- ▸ Sewing needle and matching sewing thread
- ▸ Rustproof pins for blocking
- ▸ Pillow forms: 16"/40.5 cm square and 16"/40.5 cm circular
- ▸ Fabric stiffener or spray starch (optional)

PATTERN ESSENTIALS

2 tr-cl (2 treble cluster)
[(Yarnover) two times, insert hook into stitch indicated and pull up a loop, (yarnover, pull through two loops on hook) two times] two times, yarnover and pull through all three loops on hook.

3 tr-cl (3 treble cluster)
[(Yarnover) two times, insert hook into stitch indicated and pull up a loop, (yarnover, pull through two loops on hook) two times] three times, yarnover and pull through all four loops on hook.

picot-3
Ch 3, slip st in 3rd ch from hook.

picot-4
Ch 4, slip st in 4th ch from hook.

picot-5
Ch 5, slip st in 5th ch from hook.

tight picot-3
Ch 3, slip st in st at base of chain just made.

tr2tog (treble crochet 2 stitches together)
(Yarnover) two times, insert hook in next stitch indicated and pull up a loop, (yarnover and pull through 2 loops on hook) two times; (yarnover) two times, insert hook in next stitch indicated and pull up a loop (yarnover and pull through 2 loops on hook) two times, yarnover and pull through all 3 loops on hook.

• PROJECT NOTES •

▶ The snowflake motifs are stitched separately and appliquéd/applied to the pillow.

▶ Snowflakes may be lightly starched to aid in blocking and sewing.

Giant Snowflake

Chain 6, join with slip st to form a ring.

RND 1: Ch 4 (counts as tr), tr in ring, (ch 3, 2 tr in ring) five times, ch 1, join with hdc to top of ch-4. (12 tr and 6 ch-3 spaces)

RND 2: Ch 4, tr in same space, *ch 3, (2 tr, ch 3, 2 tr) in next space; rep from * four more times, ch 3, 2 tr in beginning space, ch 1, join with hdc to top of ch-4.

RND 3: Ch 4, 2 tr in same space, ch 5, skip next space, *(3 tr, ch 3, 3 tr) in next space, ch 5, skip next space; rep from * four more times, 3 tr in beginning space, ch 1, join with hdc to top of ch-4.

RND 4: Ch 4, 2 tr in same space, ch 1, (tr, ch 3, tr) in next space, ch 1, *(3 tr, ch 3, 3 tr) in next space, ch 1, (tr, ch 3, tr) in next space, ch 1; rep from * four more times, 3 tr in beginning space, ch 1, join with hdc to top of ch-4.

RND 5: Ch 4, 3 tr in same space, ch 2, skip next ch-1 space, (tr, ch 3, tr) in next ch-3 space, ch 2, skip next ch-1 space, *(4 tr, ch 3, 4 tr) in next ch-3 space, ch 2, skip next ch-1 space, (tr, ch 3, tr) in next ch-3 space, ch 2, skip next ch-1 space; rep from * four more times, 4 tr in beginning space, ch 1, join with hdc to top of ch-4.

RND 6: Ch 4, 3 tr in same space, ch 4, skip next space, (tr, ch 3, tr) in next space, ch 4, skip next space, *(4 tr, ch 4, 4 tr) in next ch-3 space, ch 4, (tr, ch 3, tr) in next space, ch 4, skip next space; rep from * four more times, 4 tr in beginning space, ch 1, join with hdc to top of ch-4.

RND 7: Ch 4 (counts as tr), 3 tr in same space, ch 6, (tr, ch 3, tr) in next space, ch 6, skip next space, *(4 tr, ch 4, 4 tr) in next ch-3 space, ch 6, (tr, ch 3, tr) in next space, ch 6, skip next space; rep from * four more times, 4 tr in beginning space, ch 2, join with hdc to top of ch-4.

RND 8: Ch 4 (counts as tr), 4 tr in same space, ch 7, skip next space, (tr, ch 3, tr) in next space, ch 7, skip next space, *(5 tr, ch 4, 5 tr) in next ch-3 space, ch 7, skip next space, (tr, ch 3, tr) in next space, ch 7, skip next space; rep from * four more times, 5 tr in beginning space, ch 2, join with hdc to top of ch-4.

RND 9: Ch 4 (counts as tr), 4 tr in same space, *ch 8, skip next space, (tr, ch 2, picot-3, ch 3, tr) in next space, ch 8, skip next space**, (5 tr, ch 4, 5 tr) in next ch-3 space, pm in last tr made, [turn, skip first tr, slip st in next 4 tr and in ch-4 space, ch 4 (counts as tr), (4 tr, ch 4, 5 tr) in same space] four times, turn, skip first tr, slip st in next 4 tr and in ch-4 space, ch 4, (4 tr, ch 2, picot-3, ch 3, 5 tr) in same space; fasten off (*spoke made*). With RS facing, join yarn with slip st in marked tr of first shell in spike, remove marker; repeat from * around, ending last repeat at **, 5 tr in beginning space, ch 4, join with slip st in top of ch-4, turn, ch 4 (counts as tr), (4 tr, ch 4, 5 tr) in same space, [turn, skip first tr, slip st in next 4 tr and in ch-4 space, ch 4 (counts as tr), (4 tr, ch 4, 5 tr) in same space] three times, turn, skip first tr, slip st in next 4 tr and in ch-4 space, ch 4, (4 tr, ch 2, picot-3, ch 3, 5 tr) in same space; fasten off (*final spoke made*).

▶ Weave in ends.

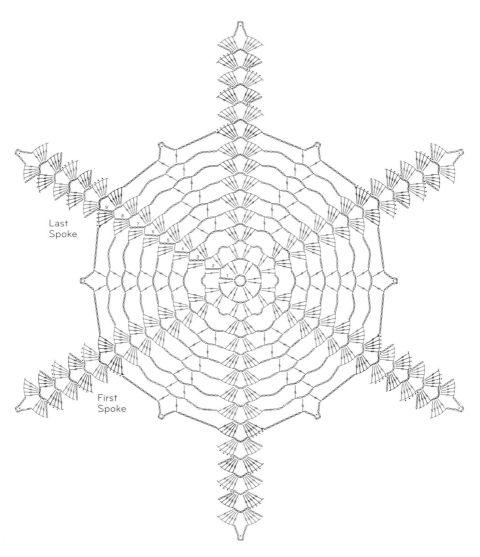

Last
Spoke

First
Spoke

GIANT SNOWFLAKE

Thread Snowflake №1

Chain 6, join with slip st to form a ring.

RND 1: Ch 1, (sc in ring, ch 8) five times, ch 4, join with tr in first sc. (6 sc and 6 ch-8 spaces)

RND 2: Ch 1, sc in same space, *ch 5, (sc, ch 5, sc) in next ch-8 space; rep from * four times, ch 5, sc in next ch-8 space, ch 5, join with slip st to first sc. (12 ch-5 spaces)

RND 3: Slip st in next 3 ch, ch 4 (counts as tr), (tr, ch 2, picot-3, ch 3, 2 tr) in same space, *ch 5, skip 1 ch-5 space, (2 tr, ch 2, picot-3, ch 3, 2 tr) in next space; rep from * four more times, ch 5, join with slip st to first sc.

▸ Fasten off. Weave in ends.

Thread Snowflake №2

▸ Chain 6, join with slip st to form a ring.

RND 1: Ch 3 (counts as dc), dc in ring, ch 2, (2 dc in ring, ch 2) five times, join with slip st in top of ch-3. (12 dc and 6 ch-2 spaces)

RND 2: Ch 4 (counts as tr), tr in same st, 2 tr in next dc, ch 2, *(2 tr in next dc) two times, ch 2; rep from * around, join with slip st in top of ch-4.

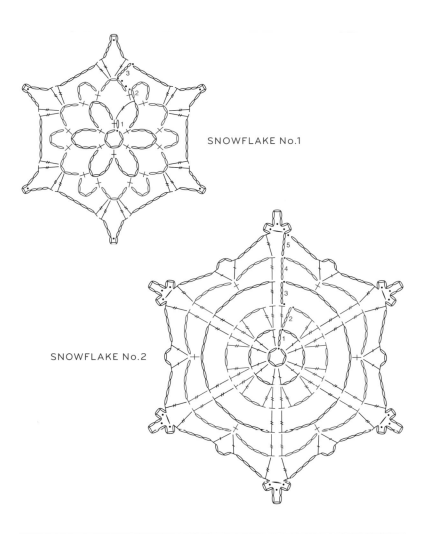

SNOWFLAKE No.1

SNOWFLAKE No.2

RND 3: Slip st in next tr, ch 4 (counts as tr), *tr in next tr, ch 7, skip 2 tr, tr in next tr; rep from * around, omitting last tr, join with slip st in top of ch-4.

RND 4: Ch 4 (counts as tr), *tr in next tr, ch 5, sc in next space, ch 5, tr in next tr; rep from * around, omitting last tr, join with slip st in top of ch-4.

RND 5: Ch 4 (counts as tr) *picot-3, picot-5, picot-3, slip st in same ch as first picot-3, tr in next tr, ch 4, (dc, ch 3, dc) in next sc, ch 4, tr in next tr; rep from * around, omitting last tr, join with slip st in top of ch-4.

▸ Fasten off. Weave in ends.

Thread Snowflake №3

▸ Chain 6, join with slip st to form a ring.

RND 1: Ch 1, (sc in ring, ch 9) five times, sc in ring, ch 5, join with tr to first sc. (6 sc and 6 ch-9 spaces)

RND 2: Ch 1, sc in same space, (ch 10, sc in next space) five times, ch 7, join with dc to first sc. (6 ch-10 spaces)

RND 3: Ch 1, sc in same space, *ch 5, picot-3, ch 6, sc in next space, ch 5, picot-3, picot-5, picot-3, slip st in same ch as first picot-3, ch 6, sc in same space; rep from * around, omitting last sc, join with slip st to first sc.

▸ Fasten off. Weave in ends.

SNOWFLAKE No.3

Thread Snowflake №4

- Chain 8, join with slip st to form a ring.

RND 1: Ch 1, 12 sc in ring, join with slip st to first sc. (12 sc)

RND 2: Ch 4, 2-tr cluster in same st, ch 8, skip 1 sc, *3-tr cl in next st, ch 8, skip 1 sc; rep from * around, join with slip st in top of first cluster. (6 ch-8 spaces)

RND 3: Ch 1, *4 sc in next ch-8 space, ch 2, picot-3, ch 3, (picot-5) two times, slip st in same ch as first picot-5, ch 3, picot-3, slip st in same ch as first picot-3, ch 2, 4 sc in same ch-8 space; repeat from * around, join with slip st in first sc.

- Fasten off. Weave in ends.

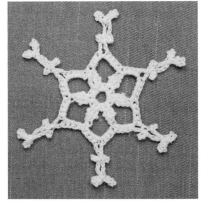

SNOWFLAKE No.4

Thread Snowflake №5

Chain 8, join with slip st to form a ring.

RND 1: Ch 4 (counts as tr), tr in ring, ch 7, (2 tr in ring, ch 7) five times, join with slip st to first sc. (12 tr and 6 ch-7 spaces)

RND 2: Ch 1, sc between first 2 tr, *ch 3, sc in next space, (ch 4, sc in same space) three times, ch 3, sc between next 2 tr; rep from * around, omitting last sc, join with slip st in first sc.

▶ Fasten off. Weave in ends.

SNOWFLAKE No.5

Thread Snowflake №6

Chain 6, join with slip st to form a ring.

RND 1: Ch 4 (counts as tr), tr in ring, ch 5, (2 tr in ring, ch 5) five times, join with slip st to top of ch-4. (12 tr and 6 ch-5 spaces)

RND 2: Ch 4, tr in next tr (counts as tr2tog), *tight picot-3, ch 5, sc in next space, ch 5, tr2tog over next 2 tr; rep from * around, omitting last tr2tog, join with slip st in top of first cluster.

▸ Fasten off. Weave in ends.

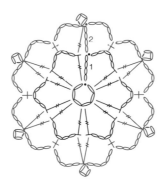

SNOWFLAKE No.6

Thread Snowflake №7

Chain 6, join with slip st to form a ring.

RND 1: Ch 4 (counts as tr), tr in ring, (ch 5, 2 tr in ring) five times, ch 2, join with dc to top of ch-4. (12 tr and 6 ch-5 spaces)

RND 2: Ch 1, (sc, ch 20, sc) in same space, ch 5, *(sc, ch 20, sc) in next space, ch 5; rep from * around, join with slip st to first sc. (6 ch-20 spaces and 6 ch-5 spaces)

RND 3: *[Sc, (ch 3, 3 sc) six times, ch 3, sc] in next ch-20 space, sc in next ch-5 space; rep from * around, join with slip st to first sc.

▶ Fasten off. Weave in ends.

SNOWFLAKE No.7

Thread Snowflake №8

Chain 10, join with slip st to form a ring.

RND 1: Ch 1, *sc in ring, (ch 2, picot-4) four times, picot-5, picot-4, skip last picot-5, slip st in same st as previous picot-4 (slip st in next 2 ch, picot-4, slip st in base of picot-4 opposite) three times, slip st in next 2 ch, sc in ring, ch 30; rep from * five more times, join with slip st in first sc.

▸ Fasten off. Weave in ends.

SNOWFLAKE No.8

Finishing

▸ **BLOCKING:** Copy the template provided on the facing page, enlarging it as necessary. Cover the template and blocking surface with plastic wrap. Dampen snowflake, stretching out each spoke of the snowflake evenly; pin in place using rust-proof pins. (If desired, use spray starch or fabric stiffener, following directions on the label). Allow to dry completely.

▸ **ROUND PILLOW:** Cut two circles with a 17"/43 cm diameter. Pin giant snowflake onto right side of one circle. Handsew in place, taking stitches along each spoke and along each chain loop in each round of snowflake. Pin right sides of two fabric circles together. Using a ½"/1.25 cm seam allowance, sew around circumference of circles, leaving a 10"/25 cm opening. Clip seams. Turn pillow cover inside out and press seams, being careful not to press snowflake. Insert pillow form into cover and sew opening closed.

▸ **SQUARE PILLOW:** Cut two 17"/43 cm squares. Pin snowflakes onto right side of one square in desired pattern. Handsew securely in place, taking care to tack down ends of each piece, as well as centers. Pin right sides of two fabric squares together. Using a ½"/1.25 cm seam allowance, sew around three sides of square. Clip corners. Turn pillow cover inside out and press seams, being careful not to press snowflakes. Insert pillow form into cover and sew opening closed.

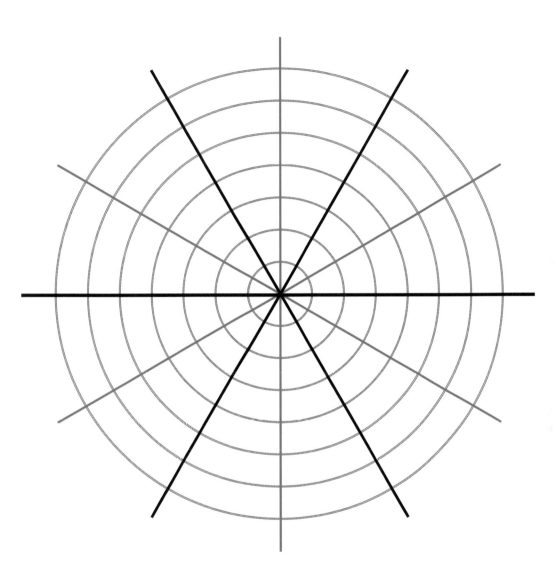

SNOWFLAKE PILLOWS TEMPLATE

Abbreviations

2tr-cl	2 treble cluster
3dtr-cluster	3 double-treble cluster
3tr-cl	3 treble cluster
4dtr-cluster	4 double-treble cluster
b-ch	bead-chain
BLdc	back loop double crochet
BLhdc	back loop half double crochet
BLsc	back loop single crochet
BLsc2tog	back loop single crochet two together
BLsc-dec	back loop single crochet decrease
BPdc	back post double crochet
BPhdc	back post half double crochet
ch	chain
dc	double crochet
dtr	double treble crochet
FLdc	front loop double crochet
FLsc	front loop single crochet
FPdc	front post double crochet
FPhdc	front post half double crochet
FPtr	front post treble crochet
hdc	half double crochet
pb	place bead
pm	place marker
rep	repeat
rnd	round

RS	right side of work
sc	single crochet
sc2tog	single crochet two together
sc3tog	single crochet three together
sc5tog	single crochet five together
sc-dec	single crochet decrease
slip st	slip stitch
st(s)	stitch(es)
tr	treble crochet
TSS	Tunisian simple stitch
TSS2tog	Tunisian simple stitch two together
WS	wrong side of work
yo	yarnover hook

Symbol Key

- **⬮** = chain (ch)
- **⬯** = work into ch not space
- **•** = slip st (sl st)
- **+** = single crochet (sc)
- **T** = half double crochet (hdc)
- **T** = double crochet (dc)
- **T** = treble crochet (tr)
- **T** = double treble crochet (dtr)
- **T** = BPdc
- **T** = FPdc
- **T** = front post treble crochet (FPtr)
- **⋀** = sc2tog
- **⋀** = sc3tog
- **⋀** = sc5tog
- **T** = 2-tr cluster

- = 3-tr cluster
- = 3dtr-cl
- = 4dtr-cl
- = popcorn
- = tight picot-2
- = picot-3
- = picot-5
- **●** = bead
- = bead chain (b-ch)
- = bead picot-3
- **⌒** = worked in back loop
- **⌣** = worked in front loop
- **◎** = magic ring
- **✳** = marker
- ⟶ / ⟵ = directional arrows
- = placement of st

170

Glossary

2TR-CL (2 TREBLE CLUSTER) [(Yarnover) two times, insert hook into stitch indicated and pull up a loop, (yarnover, pull through two loops on hook) two times] two times, yarnover and pull through all three loops on hook.

3DTR-CL (3 DOUBLE TREBLE CLUSTER) [(Yarnover) three times, insert hook into stitch indicated and pull up a loop, (yarnover, pull through two loops on hook) three times] three times, yarnover and pull through all four loops on hook.

3TR-CL (3 TREBLE CLUSTER) [(Yarnover) two times, insert hook into stitch indicated and pull up a loop, (yarnover, pull through two loops on hook) two times] three times, yarnover and pull through all four loops on hook.

4DTR-CL (4 DOUBLE TREBLE CLUSTER) [(Yarnover) three times, insert hook into stitch indicated and pull up a loop, (yarnover, pull through two loops on hook) three times] four times, yarnover and pull through all five loops on hook.

ADJUSTABLE RING (MAGIC LOOP) Leaving a 6"/15 cm tail, form a loop in the yarn and hold it in your nondominant hand with the working yarn over your index finger (A). Draw the working yarn through the loop so you have 1 loop on the hook.

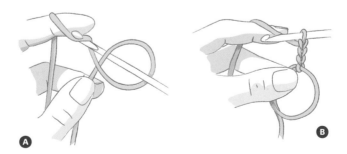

(continued on next page)

Adjustable Ring (Magic Loop), continued

Work the appropriate number of build-up chains for the first stitch (B). Then, work stitches into the ring as instructed (e.g., single, double, or treble crochet), working each stitch over the loop yarn and the tail yarn (C and D). When you've crocheted the last stitch, separate the tail from the loop and pull it up to close the loop. You may leave an open hole in the center or pull it up tightly to close the ring.

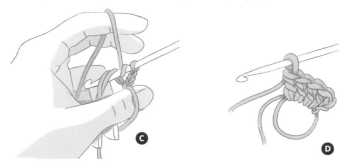

BACK LOOP, FRONT LOOP The back loop is the one farther away as you look at the work. The front loop is the one closer to you.

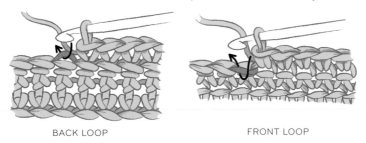

BACK LOOP   FRONT LOOP

BACK POST, FRONT POST To work a back post stitch, insert the hook from back to front to back around the post indicated (A).
To work a front post stitch, insert the hook from front to back to front around the post indicated (B).

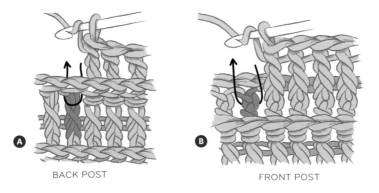

BACK POST   FRONT POST

B-CH (BEAD CHAIN) Yarnover, push bead up to hook, pull yarn through loop on hook.

BEAD PICOT-3 Ch 1, yarnover, push bead up to hook, pull yarn through loop on hook, ch 1, slip st in 3rd ch from hook.

BLDC (BACK LOOP DOUBLE CROCHET) Work 1 double crochet into the back loop only.

BLHDC (BACK LOOP HALF DOUBLE CROCHET) Work 1 half double crochet into the back loop only.

BLSC (BACK LOOP SINGLE CROCHET) Work 1 single crochet into the back loop only.

BLSC2TOG (BACK LOOP SINGLE CROCHET 2 STITCHES TOGETHER) (Insert hook into back loop of next st and pull up a loop) two times, yarnover and pull through all 3 loops on hook.

BLSC-DEC (BACK LOOP SINGLE CROCHET DECREASE) In the 2 stitches indicated, insert hook from front to back through back loop only of first stitch and from back to front through back loop only of 2nd stitch, yarnover and pull up a loop, yarnover and pull through both loops.

BPDC (BACK POST DOUBLE CROCHET) Yarnover, insert hook from back to front to back around post of stitch indicated and pull up a loop, (yarnover and pull through two loops on hook) two times.

BPHDC (BACK POST HALF DOUBLE CROCHET) Yarnover, insert hook from back to front to back around post of stitch indicated and pull up a loop, yarnover and pull through three loops on hook.

CH (CHAIN) Yarnover, pull through loop on hook.

DC (DOUBLE CROCHET) Yarnover, insert hook into stitch or space indicated and pull up a loop, (yarnover, pull yarn through two loops on hook) two times.

DTR (DOUBLE TREBLE) (Yarnover) three times, insert hook into stitch or space indicated and pull up a loop, (yarnover and pull through two loops on hook) four times.

FLDC (FRONT LOOP DOUBLE CROCHET) Work 1 double crochet into the front loop only.

FLSC (FRONT LOOP SINGLE CROCHET) Work 1 single crochet into the front loop only.

FPDC (FRONT POST DOUBLE CROCHET) Yarnover, insert hook from front to back to front around post of stitch indicated and pull up a loop, (yarnover and pull through two loops on hook) two times.

FPHDC (FRONT POST HALF DOUBLE CROCHET) Yarnover, insert hook from front to back to front around post of stitch indicated and pull up a loop, yarnover and pull through three loops on hook.

FPTR (FRONT POST TREBLE CROCHET) (Yarnover) two times, insert hook from front to back to front around post of stitch indicated and pull up a loop, (yarnover and pull through two loops on hook) three times.

HDC (HALF DOUBLE CROCHET) Yarnover, insert hook into stitch or space indicated and pull up a loop (3 loops on hook), yarnover and pull through all 3 loops on hook.

PICOT-3 Ch 3, slip st in 3rd ch from hook. (*See also* tight picot.)

PICOT-4 Ch 4, slip st in 4th ch from hook.

PICOT-5 Ch 5, slip st in 4th ch from hook.

PLACE BEAD (PB) Drop loop from hook, insert steel hook through bead and into dropped loop, pull loop through bead and snug bead up to last stitch completed, replace loop onto hook.

POPCORN Make 4 dc in one st, remove hook from loop, insert hook from front to back in first dc of group, then into dropped loop, yarnover and draw through both loops on hook.

SC (SINGLE CROCHET) Insert hook into stitch or space indicated, yarnover, pull up a loop (2 loops on hook), yarnover and pull through both loops on hook.

SC2TOG (SINGLE CROCHET 2 STITCHES TOGETHER) (Insert hook into next st and pull up a loop) two times, yarnover and pull through all 3 loops on hook.

SC3TOG (SINGLE CROCHET 3 STITCHES TOGETHER) (Insert hook into next st and pull up a loop) three times, yarnover and pull through all 4 loops on hook.

SC5TOG (SINGLE CROCHET 5 STITCHES TOGETHER) (Insert hook into next st and pull up a loop) five times, yarnover and pull through all 6 loops on hook.

SC-CL (SINGLE CROCHET CLUSTER) Insert hook in same st and pull up a loop, (insert hook in next st or space and pull up a loop) two times, yarnover and pull through all 4 loops on hook.

SC-DEC (SINGLE CROCHET DECREASE) In the 2 stitches indicated, insert hook from front to back through first stitch and from back to front through 2nd stitch, yo and pull up a loop, yo and pull through both loops.

SLIP ST (SLIP STITCH) Insert hook into stitch or space indicated, yarnover and pull through both loops on hook.

STANDING BLDC (STANDING BACK LOOP DOUBLE CROCHET) Beginning with slip knot on hook, yarnover, insert hook into back loop only of stitch indicated, yarnover, pull up a loop, (yarnover and pull through 2 loops on hook) two times.

STANDING BLSC (STANDING BACK LOOP SINGLE CROCHET) Beginning with slip knot on hook, insert hook into back loop only of stitch indicated, yarnover, pull up a loop, yarnover and pull through both loops on hook.

STANDING DC (STANDING DOUBLE CROCHET) Beginning with slip knot on hook, yarnover, insert hook into stitch or space indicated, yarnover, pull up a loop, (yarnover and pull through 2 loops on hook) two times.

STANDING SC (STANDING SINGLE CROCHET) Beginning with slip knot on hook, insert hook into stitch or space indicated, yarnover, pull up a loop, yarnover and pull through both loops on hook.

SURFACE CHAIN *Holding yarn on wrong side of fabric, insert hook from front to back through crocheted fabric and pull up a loop through fabric and through loop on hook. Repeat from * as desired.

TIGHT PICOT-2 Ch 2, slip st in stitch at base of chain.

TIGHT PICOT-3 Ch 3, slip st in st at base of chain just made.

TR (TREBLE CROCHET) (Yarnover) two times, insert hook into stitch or space indicated, pull up a loop (4 loops on hook), (yarnover and pull through 2 loops on hook) three times.

TSS (TUNISIAN SIMPLE STITCH)
Chain desired number.
Row 1: Insert hook in 2nd ch from hook, yarnover and pull up a loop, (insert hook into next ch, yarnover, pull up a loop) across (*forward pass complete*); yarnover, pull through 1 loop on hook, (yarnover, pull through 2 loops on hook) until 1 loop remains (*return pass complete*).
Row 2: Skip first vertical bar, insert hook under next vertical bar, yarnover, pull up loop (insert hook under next vertical bar, yarnover, pull up loop) across; work loops off using return pass as for Row 1. Rep Row 2 for pattern.

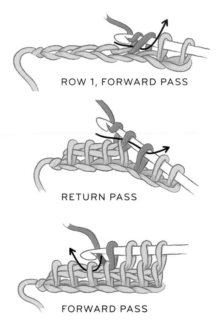

ROW 1, FORWARD PASS

RETURN PASS

FORWARD PASS

OTHER TECHNIQUES

CHANGING TO A NEW COLOR. To change yarn colors at the end of a row without fastening off the old color, work the last stitch in the old color as a partial stitch, stopping when two loops remain on the hook. Work the last "yarnover, pull through two loops on hook" with the new color, then continue with the new color. To change colors at the end of a round, work the joining slip stitch in the new color.

FELTING. Place item in a pillowcase, and close it with a rubber band. Place the pillowcase in the washing machine with pair of old jeans to add to the agitation. Set the washing machine to the hottest temperature and lowest water level. Add a small amount of soap, and begin the wash cycle. Before the cycle ends, stop the machine and check the felting progress. If more is needed, reset the wash cycle and continue. It's important to check the felting progress often, every five to ten minutes, to ensure you get the desired size.

STRINGING BEADS ONTO YARN. Use a specially designed big-eye beading needle, or use a do-it-yourself threader made from sewing thread. Here's how:

1. Thread a 6-inch length of sewing thread onto a sewing needle. Tie the ends together in a tight overhand knot.

2. Place the end of the yarn into the loop formed by the thread.

3. Using the sewing needle, pick up several beads at a time and allow them to fall down the needle and thread to the yarn.

4. With your fingers, carefully pull the beads down over the spot where the yarn and the thread cross, then down onto the yarn.

Continue picking up beads and sliding them onto the yarn until all the beads are strung.

TWISTED CORD. Cut two or more strands of yarn at least three times the desired finished length. Place an overhand knot at each end of the bundle of yarn (A). Put a crochet hook or pencil into one end to act as a handle. Slip the other end over a hook or doorknob, or have someone hold one end (B). Using the "handle," twist the yarn until it becomes tight. Pinch the yarn at the halfway point and bring the knotted ends together, allowing the cord to twist on itself (C). Carefully untie the knot and retie the strands together at each end.

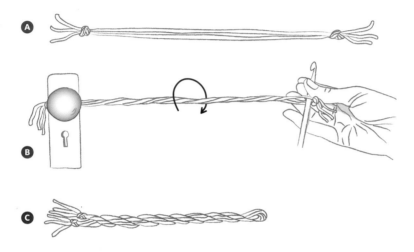

USING MARKERS IN ROUNDS. Place marker at the first stitch of the round and move it up as you work the rounds.

WORKING INTO BACK BUMP OF CHAIN. With the wrong side of the chain facing, insert hook into the bumps on the back of the chain. (The right side of the chain is a series of Vs.)

Guide to Yarn Weights

This system of categorizing yarn, gauge ranges, and recommended needle and hook sizes was developed by the Craft Yarn Council and was used to classify the yarns in this book.

	TYPES OF YARN	STITCHES IN 4" (10 CM)	RECOMMENDED HOOK SIZE
0	10–count crochet thread, lace,* fingering	32–42 dc	steel 6, 7, 8 (1.6–1.4 mm), regular B/1 (2.25 mm)
1	Sock, fingering, baby	21–32 sc	B/1 to E/4 (2.25–3.5 mm)
2	Sport, baby	16–20 sc	E/4 to 7 (3.5–4.5 mm)
3	DK, light worsted	12–17 sc	7 to I/9 (4.5–5.5 mm)
4	Worsted	11–14 sc	I/9 to K/10½ (5.5–6.5 mm)
5	Chunky, craft	8–11 sc	K/10½ to M/13 (6.5–9 mm)

* Lace weight yarns are usually crocheted on larger hooks to create lacy openwork patterns. Accordingly, a gauge range is difficult to determine. Always follow the gauge stated in your pattern.

Acknowledgments

Thanks to the suppliers of yarn and buttons: Berroco (www.berroco.com), Brown Sheep Company (brownsheep.com), Cascade Yarns (www.cascadeyarns.com), Classic Elite Yarns (www.classiceliteyarns.com), Imperial Yarn (www.imperialyarn.com), JHB International (www.buttons.com), Lion Brand Yarn (www.lionbrand.com), Tahki Stacy Charles (www.tahkistacycharles.com), Plymouth Yarn Company (www.plymouthyarn.com), Red Heart Yarn (www.redheart.com), Universal Yarn (www.universalyarn.com).

Thanks to the guest designers who contributed designs: Andee Graves, Barbara Kreuter, Kristin Omdahl, and Carol Ventura.

Thanks to the stitchers who helped us out: Rachel Ballew, Cristin Berrafato, Kristy Lucas, Barbara Kreuter (again!), Susan Heyn, and Claudia Wittmann.

Thanks to the wordsy and artsy types who did the heavy lifting: Gwen Steege, Karen Manthey, Jessica Armstrong, Alexandra Grablewski, Katrina Loving, Ilona Sherratt, Nancy Wood, and Eileen Clawson.

Contributing Designers

BARBARA KREUTER (Snowstorm Stocking, page 39; Beautiful Bows, page 118) Located in the Shenandoah Valley, where she has a lot of yarn, Barbara Kreuter uses yarn for crochet, for knitting, and for passementerie. Her online home is mabel-mabel.com.

CAROL VENTURA (Candy Cane Stocking, page 70) In the 1970s Carol Ventura fell in love with the colorful shoulder bags tapestry-crocheted by Mayan men in Guatemala. She's been exploring the potential of the technique ever since, developing new three-dimensional shapes and a system for graphing motifs. Her website www.tapestrycrochet.com includes links to tutorials, patterns, books, and videos, including free special tapestry crochet graph paper.

KRISTIN OMDAHL (Angel Ornaments, page 96) Prolific designer Kristin Omdahl works out of her home base in Florida. Learn more about her at www.styledbykristin.com.

ANDEE GRAVES (Bird Trio, page 102) Andee Graves is a self-confessed geek with a passion for math, medical science, art, design, and dark chocolate. She has been crocheting most of her life and loves to design quick sculptural pieces. She lives in the mountains of Colorado with her husband, two sons, and a changing menagerie of dogs and cats. You can read more about her design journey at http://mamas2hands.wordpress.com.

Index

Italics indicates an illustration or photo; **bold** indicates a table or pattern chart.

ALSO BY EDIE ECKMAN

Around the Corner Crochet Borders

A colorful collection of 150 crochet borders with clear instructions, charts, and color photographs.

320 pages. Paper. ISBN 978-1-60342-538-4.

Beyond the Square Crochet Motifs

Over 140 unique motif designs, from circles and stars to triangles and hexagons.

208 pages. Hardcover with concealed wire-o. ISBN 978-1-60342-039-6.

Connect the Shapes Crochet Motifs

A dazzling array of 101 motif designs and directions on how to combine multiples of a motif to create a whole new pattern.

272 pages. Hardcover with concealed wire-o. ISBN 978-1-60342-973-3.

The Crochet Answer Book, 2nd edition

With all the information crocheters need to unsnarl any project, this essential reference has been revised and expanded to answer all the questions every crocheter asks.

400 pages. Flexibind with cloth spine. ISBN 978-1-61212-406-3.

Crochet One-Skein Wonders

edited by Judith Durant & Edie Eckman

The one-skein craze meets crochet with 101 designs for bags, scarves, gloves, toys, hats, and more, each using just a single skein of yarn.

288 pages. Paper. ISBN 978-1-61212-042-3.

These and other books from Storey Publishing are available wherever quality books are sold or by calling 1-800-441-5700. Visit us at www.storey.com or sign up for our newsletter at www.storey.com/signup.